PACIFIC TROLLER

PACIFIC TROLLER

LIFE ON THE NORTHWEST FISHING GROUNDS

FRANCIS E. CALDWELL

ALASKA NORTHWEST PUBLISHING COMPANY
ANCHORAGE, ALASKA

*In memory of the humble and brave
men who have hopefully outfitted their
vessels, bid family and friends a cheery
farewell, sailed off into the vast
reaches of the Pacific in search of the
salmon and the tuna and have never
been heard from again.*

Second printing 1978

Library of Congress cataloging in publication data:
Caldwell, Francis E
    Pacific troller
      1.   Fishermen—North Pacific Ocean.
2.   Trolling (Fishing)   3.   Pacific salmon fisheries
—Northwest, Pacific.   I.   Title.
SH214.4.C34   338.3'72'5091643   77-10324
ISBN 0-88240-099-1

The Epilogue "The Price of Fish" is reprinted
with permission from *The Portland Oregonian*
and *National Fisherman/Pacific Fisherman.*

Photographs by the author, except as noted
Design by Dianne Hofbeck
CartoGraphics and diagrams by Jon.Hersh

Alaska Northwest Publishing Company
Box 4-EEE, Anchorage, Alaska 99509

Printed in U.S.A.

Contents

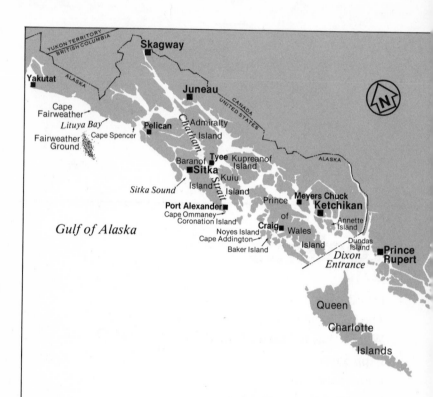

Cape Fairweather to Cape Foulweather

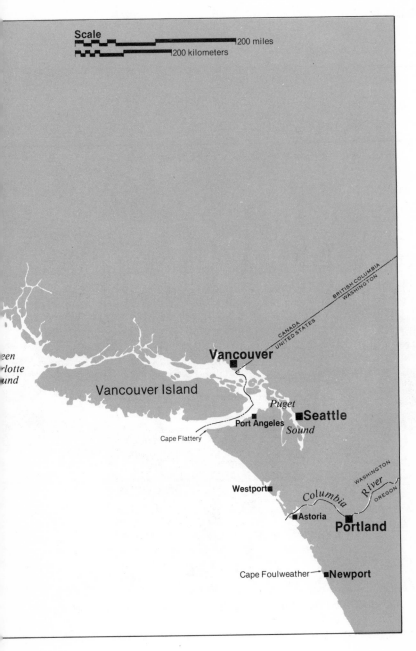

Scale

200 miles

200 kilometers

een
rlotte
und

Vancouver

CANADA
UNITED STATES

BRITISH COLUMBIA
WASHINGTON

Vancouver Island

Puget

Seattle

Port Angeles

Sound

Cape Flattery

Westport

Columbia

River

WASHINGTON
OREGON

Astoria

Portland

Cape Foulweather

Newport

A forest of poles. The offshore trolling fleet packs the moorings at Sitka, Alaska.

Introduction

Cape Fairweather, Alaska, lies about 15°, or 900 miles, up the coast from Cape Foulweather, which is just south of Depoe Bay, Oregon. Captain James Cook named Fairweather in 1778, either after a Captain Fairweather or because of climatic conditions at the time of discovery. If the latter, most mariners would agree that the cape was poorly named. Cook just happened by on an unusual day.

Cape Fairweather is 60 miles north of Cape Spencer, where the Inside Passage ends and the open ocean of the Gulf of Alaska begins. The cape is unpretentious, an evenly rounded point, long and low in elevation. A slight indentation behind it gives a whisper of protection from southeasterly winds. Salmon trollers driven from the Fairweather grounds, 50 miles offshore, frequently anchor behind the cape when the dangerous bar at the entrance to sheltered Lituya Bay, 15 miles to the south, is impassable.

The land near Cape Fairweather, covered with stunted spruce whose tops lean away from the prevailing southeast winds, is glacial moraine strewn with large boulders. Majestic Mt. Fairweather juts 15,320 feet into the heavens behind the cape, wearing a perennial snowcap. The cape's only inhabitants are moose, marmots, squirrels, eagles and huge brown bears.

Oregon's Cape Foulweather provides no lee for fishing boats. It is one of the windiest places along the coast, so much so there have been plans for building a plant on its summit to produce electricity from wind power. On the very top of the cape, and only a short distance from the Pacific Coast Highway, is a gift shop that clings to the steep cliffs. The manager says they sometimes are forced to flee the building because of winds, recorded as high as 140 knots, even though the shop is built almost as strong as a lighthouse.

Between these two capes are a lot of whitecaps and most of the Pacific trolling grounds. Included are the Alaskan salmon grounds, the British Columbia salmon and albacore grounds and almost half the Oregon grounds.

Most of this book was first drafted on harbor days and during long wheel watches between Capes Foulweather and Fairweather, with a "Jimmy" diesel purring beneath my feet and an iron mike grinding out its "whump, whump," as it steered. In the background, above the noise of the engine, a radio transmitter squealed about the poor fishing and the lousy weather.

This is a book about the commercial trolling business, about king and silver salmon, albacore tuna, halibut, sudden storms, flying spray, dangerous bars, the boats of the fleet and the men and women who operate them.

Dale Caldwell, the author's son, in the pilothouse whiling away the long hours of wheel watch en route to Alaska on the Laverne II. *The automatic pilot, or "Iron Mike," takes care of the actual steering when there are no dangers in the vicinity.*

The Fishermen

Every spring, migrating geese wing their way north along the Pacific seaboard. But even before they begin their long flight, West Coast salmon trollers are nervously pacing in their homes and, with the slightest excuse, rush to the waterfront and the familiar world of fish boats, marine supply stores and fellow fishermen. Forgotten are the endless days of toil on a heaving deck endured the previous season. Dimmed by months ashore are memories of long, weary nights spent jogging out gales, grabbing bites of cold food and choking down stale bread. Faded are memories of the loneliness of long months spent away from families and the discomforts of living at sea aboard small boats.

The familiar odors of pine tar and fresh paint spur the men into a frenzy of activity on their own boats. They join fellow trollers in coffee shops and beer joints, and listen to captains speculate earnestly about where the best fishing might be in the coming season. The talk, and thoughts of fresh money in the bank, drives them to work on their equipment far into the night.

Engines are overhauled and tuned. Trolling poles are peeled and festooned with wire and lines. Electronic equipment is checked and rechecked. Vital machinery is inspected. Stainless trolling wire is marked off in 4- or 5-fathom sections. And everywhere there's fresh paint—blue, black, yellow, white, gray, red and green. It's slathered on pilothouses, hulls, masts, decks and on the men themselves. Paint gets carried home on shoes, hats and truck seats. It gets into hair and eyes and finally the bathroom sink. Vessels are hauled out at marine ways to copper-paint the bottoms and replace the zinc anodes. The men hate the copper paint: it's toxic and some are wary of breathing it for fear of becoming sick.

Fishermen's wives watch these annual activities with a resigned detachment. When their husbands arrive home with copper bottom paint on their caps instead of red, white or green hull paint, the women know the men will be leaving soon. Bottom painting is the last job before the fleet sails. Wives mend heavy woolens with faraway looks in their eyes. They'll soon be alone. For some wives the waiting and loneliness will be hellish because their men may not return until autumn leaves turn brown—if indeed they return at all.

The wives listen silently to the torrent of waterfront gossip brought home each night. They ponder their place in the scheme of things. How, they wonder, can a woman compete with something so inanimate as a fish boat? They toy with their dinners. Across the table a husband is explaining why he had to spend a thousand dollars on a new loran set, but he cannot afford to have the car repaired until he gets out fishing. In the same breath he tells about the predictions of a famous fish forecaster, Emil Eckberg, that in Southeastern Alaska there will be poor fishing in April and May but June and July will be the best in 40 years. The Washington coast will be just the opposite.

A few fishermen's wives defy old customs. They pack their sea bags with jeans, sweaters and boots and go off with their men. They cook hot tasty meals on swaying galley stoves; they help clean fish, steer the boat, navigate and do countless other chores.

Those wives who remain ashore embrace their men for the last time for months. Then, amid a glow of red and green running lights and the stench of acrid diesel exhaust, the vessels vanish into the early morning mists.

The trollers in the beginning watch the instruments nervously for signs of malfunction. Engines and reduction gears are checked and listened to. Then, confident that the equipment has survived the winter in good shape, they sit back with their coffee. What a relief, they muse, to be back at sea again.

Some work their way down the coast, others up. It isn't uncommon for a man to live in Newport, Oregon (a first-rate fishing town itself), keep his boat in Port Angeles, Washington, and fish in Alaska. Vessels with Fort Bragg or Moss Landing, California, as their ports of call can be seen 1,500 miles up the coast on the Fairweather grounds in Alaska. One troller who fished out of Ketchikan lived in Norway during the winter. This, I believe, sets a record as to distance between job and home. "It doesn't matter where a troller lives," a fisherman once summed it up, "because he's seldom home in the summer anyway."

The mild climate makes Washington State's Puget Sound the favorite wintering ground for much of the fleet that operates between Capes Foulweather and Fairweather. Skippers who plan to start their season in Alaska have a 600-mile cruise through British Columbia's famed Inside Passage. They log an average of 120 miles a day and usually anchor at night in excellent harbors along the way. Watchful of gales, they keep a sharp eye on the morning sky and on the barometer. Once they've passed through Johnstone Strait, signs of spring are left behind and snow patches are seen along the wild and timbered shore. For these northbound mariners, and for the Canadians who join them on the offshore grounds of the Gulf of Alaska, spring is a long time coming and always seems just around the corner.

During blows, the boats congregate at Christie Pass and wait for calm weather to cross Queen Charlotte Sound. Farther north, they wait in Brundige Inlet, on Dundas Island, to cross Dixon Entrance. The longer it blows, the more boats congregate. Then, some morning before daylight, they'll leave with a roar of diesels, mast lights weaving and bobbing in unison on the swells leftover from the blow.

Many trollers like to start their season on the west coast of Prince of Wales Island, some 100 miles west of Ketchikan, They battle the infamous weather off Capes Bartolome, Chirikoff and Addington, and seek refuge from the savage gales in harbors such as Little Bremerton, Kelly Cove, behind Cone Island and in

Home port for the Laverne II *and Frank Caldwell's new boat, the* Donna C—*Port Angeles, Washington.*

Pigeon Pass. Storms lasting 3 to 7 days, accompanied by driving rain and wind-whipped snow, hone the men's tempers and send them in search of better harbors. But a day or two of good fishing out on the 50-fathom edge, with sooty shearwaters and petrels whirling overhead and a few shiny king salmon coming aboard, cause them to forget the discomforts.

When leaves start to appear on alders along the shore and the wind loses some of its bite, a few boats slip away to westward. Always there is the lure of better fishing elsewhere. They'll work their way to such places as Snipe Bay, Cape Edgecumbe off Sitka, Cape Cross and Cape Bingham. Some of the most ambitious, and those who have larger boats, may continue up the coast to Cape Fairweather. For most, this will be the end of the trek northwest. Few trollers venture farther. Those who do, seemingly driven by the same roving instincts that guide the salmon they seek, will try the grounds above Cape Saint Elias in Prince William Sound. The weather in these latitudes is seldom good and summer lasts but a few weeks.

About 40 miles off Cape Fairweather, a subterranean mountain range juts up from the ocean floor, with one peak a mere 78 feet from the crest of the waves. Small fish and shrimp are fond of these canyons and lurk there safe from the currents. Salmon and halibut swarm on them to feed.

It isn't enough that the fisherman know the surface of the sea, he must also know the land beneath: the rocks that lurk to rip out the bottom of his boat, the sunken reefs that can strip him of hundreds of dollars' worth of fishing gear, the submerged snags and sunken ships. He must know the hidden contours of his fishing grounds as well as the farmer knows the hills, gullies and fields of his land. Otherwise, he cannot lower 50 or 60 pounds of lead close enough to the bottom to catch salmon without losing the expensive gear.

Before the troller's eyes a fathometer winks out the depth all the while he is fishing a grabby bottom. One meter is mounted inside, where it's visible from the galley and wheelhouse. Another is mounted on the stern so the fisherman can watch it while working there.

Sometimes, in order to catch kings, it's necessary to actually bounce the leads on the bottom and around the reefs that jut up from the ocean floor. When working such grounds, constant vigilance is essential. If a fisherman becomes so absorbed in other tasks that he forgets to check the fathometer, he may suddenly find himself in 15 fathoms instead of 30. About then the poles start jerking.

The only recourse is to open the throttle wide and hope the increased speed will lift the heavy leads over the obstacle. Failing this, the leads hang up and break off. If the gear is rigged right, the breaking straps on both the tag lines and the leads will part. If not, the poles may break off, dropping a twisted maze of guy wires and rigging in the water to foul the prop, and the trolling wires may part at the blocks with a complete loss of all the gear.

The boats that sail south from Cape Flattery, Washington's northwest tip, to fish the coasts of Washington, Oregon and California have prospects of better weather. Also, they have a

Fishermen Ray Martin, Harold Newman and Ernie Shaw yarn about the weather at Moss Landing, California.

Frank Caldwell shows off a hefty king salmon aboard the Laverne II. *This one fish will pay for a healthy share of the day's expenses.*

chance to get home for a visit (known as "going home to cut the grass") once in a while. They are nearer repair yards and machine shops in case of breakdown. But they must live day and night upon the open ocean; there are few harbors along this coast. Drifting on a heavy swell is a miserable way to spend the night. The trollers working in Alaska (Fairweather grounds excluded) may take advantage of the many harbors where they can go in, drop the pick and get a good night's rest.

Many skippers have difficulty trying to decide which direction to go. It's not unusual for a boat to head for California for the April 15 opening, sail confidently down the coast as far as Astoria at the mouth of the Columbia River, have a change of heart and reverse course for Alaska. Indecision is a normal state of affairs for many trollers. Fishing is a gambling business.

If an area had a good run of fish one year there'll be swarms of boats there the next—trying, of course, to catch last year's fish. The salmon seldom cooperate. If anyone has figured out how to outguess salmon, I certainly haven't heard about it.

The commercial fisherman has contempt and pity for anyone who works at a regular job. A wage earner, in the fisherman's eyes, must perform all sorts of unbecoming tasks in his pursuit of a living. Yet the fisherman will struggle to keep his feet on a slimy, rolling deck 20 hours a day in freezing wind and rain and consider himself the salt of the earth. Day after day of complete failure will be easily and quickly forgotten when, after a few minutes' work, several hundred dollars' worth of fish lie flopping on deck.

I've known fishermen so broken in body that movement was a feat, or crushed with debt and failure and loneliness, who still considered themselves blessed to have become fishermen.

Fishermen can forget the wet, cold nights without sleep, forget the long, tiresome wheel watches, forget the battering of a gale and the miseries of living at sea on a small boat, just by musing on a certain boat once owned, or remembering a successful trip with a full hold of fish delivered.

Strangers who wander into the picturesque mooring basins along the coast and listen to the salty talk assume that fishermen are realists. They mistake straightforwardness for the rigorous practicality of natural outdoorsmen, not knowing that, by the very nature of their business, these men are true romantics.

What a Way to Make a Living!

This morning started like many others: up at first light; start the engine; pump the bilge; put the coffeepot on to boil. Next, go to the bow and begin hauling in the anchor. Around me, neighboring skippers, hunched against the morning chill, are bent over their anchor winches, kicking at the cable to spool it evenly, and having the day's first cigarette.

The anchor, caked with gooey mud and festooned with kelp, clangs against the bow. I shut off the winch and head for the warmth of the wheelhouse. The boat is free now and I must work until dusk permits me to drop anchor again.

I engage the clutch and steer carefully among other boats still lying at anchor, their poles bristling like gigantic porcupines. It's been a calm night, I've slept well and am refreshed and eager to search for the fish.

Some of the anchored vessels have lighted galleys, others remain dark. I pass the *Tuckahoe*'s familiar silhouette. Nels Nelson's shadowy form is on deck, pumping the bilge. I trip my foghorn slightly and he lifts an arm in salute.

I cruise slowly from the protection of Cone Island, off the west coast of Prince of Wales Island, where I had anchored for the night. In the channel I feel the ocean swells again. I turn on a light and peer at the instrument panel. Oil pressure, okay; generator, charging; water temperature, still cold. I must let the engine warm up. By the time I've secured the coffeepot so it won't slide and picked up a few items carelessly left on the galley table, the engine is warm and I speed up to 1,600 rpm. It's an hour's run out to the 40-fathom edge where the fish lie. The automatic pilot is working well and I set a course that will take me out to the center of Veta Bay, off Baker Island.

I lounge in the captain's chair and thrill to the sight of another new day. In the eastern sky the Master Artist is jabbing the heavens awake with dashes of pinks and reds from His brush. The sea looks oily, a lifeless gray. The clouds are brassy, tinged with pink.

Then, for a precious moment, the sun's rays reflect off the cloud cover. Suddenly I'm enveloped in a world of molten gold as Veta Bay becomes livid with reflections. Out on the edge, the sea and sky remain mated together in inky nothingness. I watch spellbound as the gold turns to copper. Then the painting vanishes. Out of the dark mysterious womb of night a sparkling new day has been born.

The swells try to roll me from my seat. I'm in the open now. My eyes sweep the bay for signs of sea birds feeding. Where will the fish be today? Will they be deep or shallow? Will they bite spoons? What kind? Or will they bite only on bait? If so, what length of leaders behind the flashers? Will I be among the fortunate few who make expenses today? Or will the run of bad luck I've been having hound me again? These are questions the salmon troller must ponder each day.

The hour's run is a time to meditate, to think of what life is all about. It's a time to dream of future plans—that hunting trip among the crimson October leaves after mule deer in Washington's Okanogan County, a new boat . . .

I haven't yet heard the sound of a human voice today, of the world and its troubles, man and his perpetual opinions, and I keep the radio turned off. It would shatter the precious spell. I cherish these few minutes before the gear is out, knowing that after those spoons hit the water I'm committed to another long day. Fragrant, fresh-boiled coffee draws me to the galley. Dark brown pumpernickel, toasted on top of the stove and smothered with butter and jam tastes good. Should the fish decide to bite it will be many hours before I'll have the opportunity to cook breakfast.

By now we're off Outer Point. We? My boat and I are a team. To the northwest, Cape Addington juts like a jagged finger into the Pacific. Three miles to the southeast the incredible pinkish cliffs of sheer, solid granite behind Cape Chirikof loom from morning shadows.

Just off the port bow hovers a cluster of gulls. The ocean erupts in a cloud of steam. A bluish black whale's back follows. After several spurts of vapor, the mammal sounds with a regal salute of its great forked tail, then disappears again beneath the gray waves.

I contemplate setting out my gear here. Why not? There are schools of needlefish showing on the surface. I hesitate, though, because I've done it before, only to be sorry. Better continue to where the fish were yesterday.

When the fathometer shows we're over 30 fathoms we sail under a canopy of birds, flocks of brownish, sooty shearwaters fluttering in a feeding frenzy. Next come black- and white-bellied petrels. They sweep around the bow of the boat like snowflakes in a blizzard. Changing course in perfect cadence, they skim the crest of each oncoming wave as if controlled by a computer. Bobbing indifferently on the surface is a trio of arctic loons. They watch us approach. When they see collision is inevitable, they paddle frantically aside and dive under the boat. They're too full of food to fly. Their dark backs with the bars of white remind me of the seersucker clothing I hated so much as a boy.

Birds are an important factor in locating fish in the ocean. I peer in all directions for my favorites, the black-legged kittiwakes. Trim little sailors with white underbodies, slate gray wings and black wing tips, the kittiwakes are infrequent visitors in Alaska, sensibly preferring the warmer climate of California's coastal waters.

A school of porpoises splashes and leapfrogs to the bow. For 10 minutes they frolic and pilot me along the way. The sea has been called lonely and foreboding, but to me it has never been lonely.

Keen Gau's Bluejacket, *seen here with trolling rig out off Cape Cross, Alaska. As is clear from her sleek lines, this fine boat is a converted yacht, but the scrap of sail shown flying is now just a "steadying sail," used to help damp excessive rolling motion. Formerly an ocean racer,* Bluejacket *carried the Gau family on a 2-year cruise of the South Pacific.*

And I can be lonely—any time I'm in a large city by myself. With millions of people within several miles I can become despondent. At sea, the birds and the animals have always been sociable. This morning, in my own private way, I thank Him for sharing His creatures with me.

My coffee cup is now empty. The fathometer shows 38 fathoms, smooth bottom. I'm nearing the edge where the fish have been prowling in search of food. I throttle down to trolling speed. It's time to go to work. The magic spell is broken.

I struggle into a woolen coat and oilskins. Outside, the west wind still carries the bite of winter. I switch from the fathometer in the pilothouse to the one aft in the trolling hatch, fix the pilot so I can operate it from aft, engage the power takeoff for the gurdies and leave the warm cabin. It's 5:15 A.M.

The fish are biting. Author's stepson, Vaughn Wilson, hurls aboard a big albacore tuna on the Laverne II.

First the lightest leads, the 25-pounders on the main lines, are lowered overboard, one at a time. Four leaders containing spoons and two with flashers and bait are snapped on the marks along the wire. When 40 fathoms are out, I tag the wire off and let it swing to the tip of the pole.

After both light leads are out I do likewise with the 50-pounders on the bow lines. Seven tiny strands of stainless steel wire, $12.50 worth of lead and another $30 worth of gear slither into the greenish, cold sea. On one line are brass and bronze #8 Superior spoons. Another line has #7 Superiors in brass, brass and copper and gold bronze. Still another holds a few Katchmores in various colors. I check each hook before I place it in the water to make sure it is needle sharp and the eye is stout. Salmon weighing up to 60 pounds lurk in Veta Bay. If I'm lucky enough to latch onto a fish that size I don't want a five-cent hook to fail. I go into the cabin and select new ones from a drawer containing several thousand hooks. I reshape them to suit me and sharpen their points.

After all four lines are out I watch the tips of the poles for action. The boat is rolling heavily. I put out the stablizers. They dangle underwater off each pole, some 15 feet from the side of the boat. The boat steadies and I glance at the tip of each pole before going inside. There is little else I can do to increase my chances.

Off comes the wool coat. The coffeepot goes back on and I huddle over the stove, letting my numb hands thaw. From where I stand I can see the ocean ahead. I must be forever on the lookout for floating kelp, logs and other debris that could break a tag line or strip the spoons off a wire. I can also see the tattletale lines that run forward. When a salmon hits a spoon, the tattletales jiggle back and forth and I can see them from inside the cabin.

While I sip coffee I turn the radio to 2182. Annette Island announces that a marine weather forecast and notice to mariners will be broadcast over 2670 in 5 minutes. The forecast is for continued light westerlies for the area from Dixon Entrance to Sitka. Weather permitting, I'll fish 4 more days before running up to Lew Scott's Tokeen Cold Storage to sell my catch. I look at my calendar, where each day I've marked the number of fish caught. There were three on the first day, seven on the second. On the third, fourth and fifth days I anchored in Pigeon Pass while a southeaster blew itself out. Yesterday, the sixth day, I caught 13 salmon. The 23 salmon, now iced in the hold, are not large fish—perhaps they weigh 300 pounds altogether. At 70 cents a pound, I'm not doing so well. My only hope of making something this trip lies in the days ahead. I peer at the tattletale lines. Nothing so far, but it's early in the day, early in the season. Many boats aren't even fishing yet. But there are those pressing bills to pay . . .

By 7 A.M. I've trolled to a position straight off Cape Chirikof. Storm-washed granite cliffs behind the cape are an excellent landmark. I come up from the engine room after checking the power takeoff. Something could have hit while I was below.

After the excitement of the catch comes the drudgery of dressing the fish. Frank Caldwell cleans a big salmon on the Donna C, *while many more wait their turn in the holding pens.*

Bundled to the eyes I go back to haul a line. I can tell by the way it pulls that there are fish on it. There are three, all about 8-pounders—but they're halibut. The season isn't open and I must release them unharmed. Already hanging on the boom is a halibut I kept for eating. Perhaps I'll have some again for dinner tonight. I'll dip halibut chunks in eggs and cracker crumbs and deep-fat fry them. Along with a salad and baked potato, it will be delicious. Supper is planned.

While running the rest of the lines, I notice three other boats coming along behind. One is the *Tuckahoe*, but I can't be sure of the rest. Up ahead are three more. They anchored in the bay behind Chirikof last night and didn't have the long run from harbor. I've been looking at the profiles of those three boats from so many different angles and in so many different places for so many years that I'd recognize them under almost any conditions. One is the *Stamsund*, the only schooner in our little fleet, another is the *Sharyn A* and the third is the *High C*. The owners are my friends. On the inside is another boat with four poles. Probably the *Argo*. The *Argo* and the *Tuckahoe* are the only boats present with four poles.

Each line I run has halibut on. I rebait and reset the lines and return to the pilothouse to switch on the CB. I recognize the voice of Perry Coburn, owner of the *High C*.

". . . hardly know what to make of this. Now we've got the weather and there's no fish. When it was blowing and we couldn't get out, they were here. It's a crazy business. Over."

"That's for sure, Perry. I don't know what to do either. I haven't had an offering yet. Just drag around and hope they bite later on, I guess."

It's Ed Allain. He and his wife Ann fish together on their *Sharyn A*. Ed started trolling with his father, "Frenchie" Allain, when Ed was only a boy. Now he is a highliner, the term we use for a good producer.

I don't feel quite so bad. I'm not the only one still skunked. But I wish I had put my gear in back by the whale. Perhaps the fish that were here yesterday moved there last night.

I'm in 56 fathoms now. I let one side of my gear down another 10 fathoms. I know what will happen; it'll catch more halibut. Sometimes the salmon are deep, though, and it's worth a try. Before I get back inside the lines begin to quiver. In disgust I haul them up, skake off the halibut and reset the lines, 36 fathoms on the bow and 40 on the mains.

It is 8 o'clock and I'm hungry. Maybe if I fix breakfast a fish will bite. You can troll for hours with nothing to do, but just as you sit down to a hot meal a fish will get on. And you've got to go haul in the salmon before a sea lion beats you to it.

A boat is approaching almost bow to bow. I recognize the *Stamsund*. Red Rawley is out in the trolling hatch, running gear.

His red woolen cap matches his complexion. Jovial, good for a laugh anytime, Red is a good fisherman, a hard worker, often first to the fishing grounds in the spring, first out in the mornings and last to go in at night. He's known as a tough dragger. I walk out on deck and wave to him. I hold my hands waist high, palms open and face up to signal "no fish." His face parts in a grin. He holds up three fingers. I see splashes of white water behind the schooner's stern. He's got another one on. I go inside and watch through the window. Red leans over, there's a fast movement and a streak of silver flashes through the air. Some guys have all the luck.

I slice bacon for the skillet. Hash-brown spuds and two eggs join the bacon. Then, over coffee, I relax in the chair and listen to 2638, the fishermen's band. I'm just in time to hear a conversation between Don Mills on the *Ann* and Frank Diner on the *Sefora*. The *Ann* is in Sitka Sound and the *Sefora* has just left Dundas Island heading for the Alaskan border.

"Have you fellows been able to get out up there?" Frank asks. His fishing grounds are in Sitka Sound and he's anxious for news.

"Oh," Don Mills replies, "we've been out to the rock pile and over to the island a couple times. I don't know what for, though. There're no fish."

"Yeah," Frank laughs, "well, there aren't supposed to be any fish until after I get there."

"If that's the case, you'd better hurry up," Don answers.

"We are. We'll be in Ketchikan tonight, Petersburg tomorrow and the Hot Springs the next. Should be seeing you in about 4 days."

I lose interest. Something, possibly a salmon, is shaking my bow line. Sea lions have been bothering us for several days and with salmon so scarce I don't want to lose one that way. I rush out without a coat.

I feel the wire as it slowly comes up. Something is jerking. My heart leaps. The first leader appears and I unhook it and coil it out of the way. The same with the second and the third. The fourth is a flasher and bait. The bait hook is empty. My heart sinks. I run the remainder. All are empty. There was a salmon on that bait, but it was poorly hooked. No use feeling bad, it happens all the time. There'll be more—I hope.

I'm numb with cold by the time I get back inside. It was foolish to rush out without a coat. A white boat is trolling out from the shore, pointed toward me. The flying bridge and the bow poles carried high identify the *Suzie M* of Bellingham. I've seen her on trolling grounds from Fairweather to Foulweather. Owner Bob Gay steps on deck, holds up five fingers, hollers and points toward Cape Addington. I can't hear him, so I give him the no fish sign and retreat inside, somewhat puzzled. Perhaps he is trying to tell me that fishing is better at Cape Addington. I don't see how it could be worse. Bob's five fish aren't many but I feel badly beaten. It's a normal, but still painful feeling. I'm often beaten.

The CB radio springs to life. "What's happening, Cap?" It's Bob Gay's familiar voice.

"It's odd that you should ask me," I reply dryly. "Which way did they go?"

"West," Bob replies. "Into Edmund Allain's hold."

"Is he slugging 'em, as usual?"

"Roger on that, Cap. When we met, he stood on deck waving his fingers at me until I was clear out of sight."

I laugh. It is good to talk to someone. "I've five fish less than you. Does Edmund have me in the sack?"

"Badly. He's got what you caught the first day of your trip."

"I see," remembering I'd caught three that day. "How can we get it fixed so's he's on some kind of quota?"

"Between him and Red the poor salmon just don't have a chance." Bob sighs and signs off.

This sort of monotony-relieving talk helps pass the long hours.

Changing gear probably won't catch any fish but it will make me feel better. Back in the stern I switch the spoons on the bow lines to #6½ brass McMahons. I remove the flashers from one main line and run all spoons. Satisfied that I've at least done something, I return to the pilothouse and prepare lunch. I open my last can of venison, make gravy and pour it over slices of bread.

I sit down to eat. Glancing up, I see the port tattletale jerking, the spring stretched way back. Then it shoots forward and is still. I set my plate aside, grab my coat and hurry aft, expecting to see the breaking strap on the tag line parted. It hasn't. Before I reach

54′ Offshore Troller

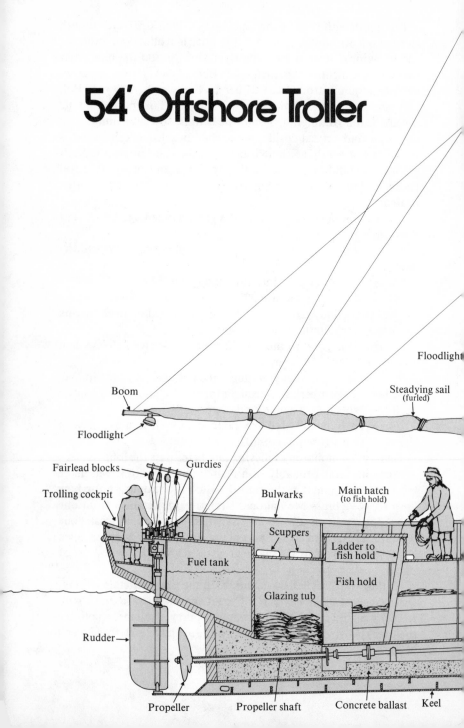

Floodlight

Boom

Steadying sail
(furled)

Floodlight

Fairlead blocks

Gurdies

Trolling cockpit

Bulwarks

Main hatch
(to fish hold)

Scuppers

Fuel tank

Ladder to
fish hold

Fish hold

Glazing tub

Rudder

Propeller

Propeller shaft

Concrete ballast

Keel

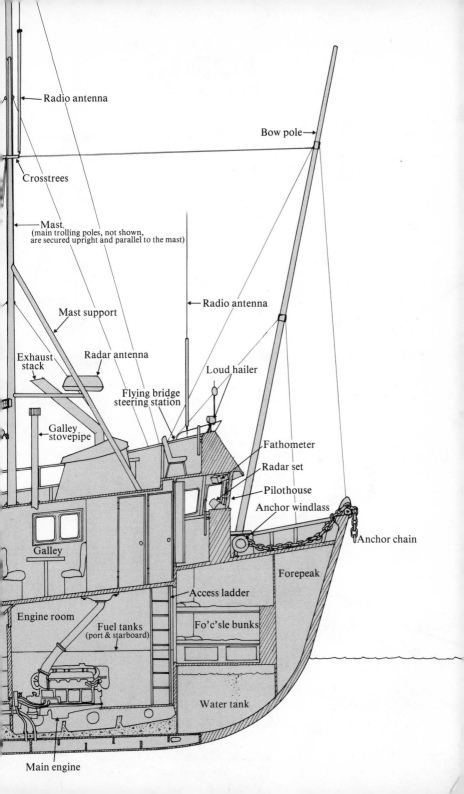

Radio antenna

Bow pole

Crosstrees

Mast,
(main trolling poles, not shown,
are secured upright and parallel to the mast)

Radio antenna

Mast support

Loud hailer

Exhaust stack

Radar antenna

Flying bridge
steering station

Galley
stovepipe

Fathometer

Radar set

Pilothouse

Anchor windlass

Galley

Anchor chain

Forepeak

Access ladder

Engine room

Fuel tanks
(port & starboard)

Fo'c'sle bunks

Water tank

Main engine

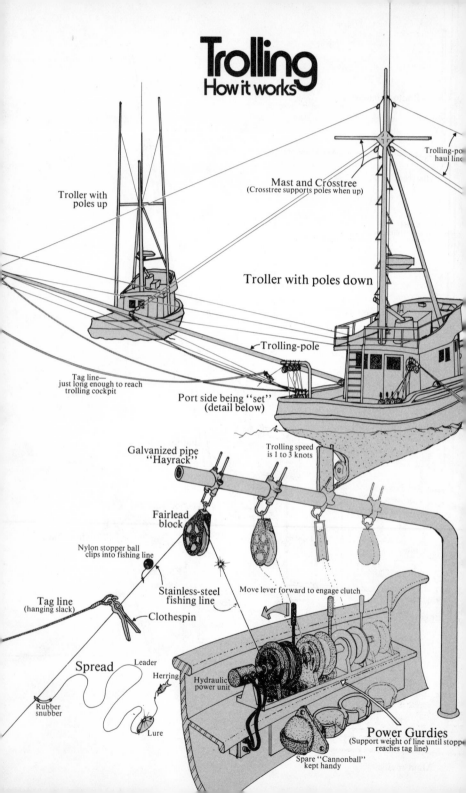

Trolling
How it works

Troller with poles up

Mast and Crosstree
(Crosstree supports poles when up)

Trolling-pole
haul line

Troller with poles down

Trolling-pole

Tag line—
just long enough to reach
trolling cockpit

Port side being "set"
(detail below)

Galvanized pipe
"Hayrack"

Trolling speed
is 1 to 3 knots

Fairlead
block

Nylon stopper ball
clips into fishing line

Move lever forward to engage clutch

Tag line
(hanging slack)

Stainless-steel
fishing line

Clothespin

Spread

Leader

Herring

Hydraulic
power unit

Rubber
snubber

Lure

Power Gurdies
(Support weight of line until stopper
reaches tag line)

Spare "Cannonball"
kept handy

A typical offshore trolling rig consists of long poles to hang the fishing lines out in the water away from the boat, and sets of gurdies (winches), usually power driven, to feed out and haul in the main lines.

Three or four tag lines hang down from each pole. These lines are static and fairly short, just able to reach the trolling cockpit in the stern of the fishing boat. At the end of each tag line is attached a bronze troller's "clothespin," a tough spring-loaded device. This device is clipped around the stainless-steel fishing line and will allow the line to run freely through it. At the point where the desired length of fishing line has been run out from the gurdie, a nylon stopper ball is clipped into the line. This ball will not pass through the "clothespin" so all the weight of the fishing line will then be taken by the tag line hanging from the pole.

To set the lines, the fisherman first lowers the poles, keeping the ends of the tag lines in the cockpit. The fishing line is payed through the clothespin and the end attached to a heavy lead weight, often called a cannonball. The cannonball, which may weigh as much as 65 pounds, holds the line down at the desired depth and is designed to break away if it snags the bottom so that the whole rig is not lost. Then the "spreads" (rubber snubber to absorb shocks, leader, lure and/or bait and hooks) are clipped onto the steel fishing line at intervals of 12 to 18 feet. The length of each leader will vary, and as many as 18 spreads may be attached to a single line.

Each line is controlled by its gurdie. As each spread is attached, the main line is fed out to the next interval at which a spread will be attached, until the chosen number are streamed. The line is then lowered to the desired depth and the nylon stopper ball is clipped on. The end of the tag line is let go and more of the fishing line is run out until the tag line hangs vertically to the water and takes the full weight.

Now the next line is set, working from the outboard end of the pole, in. A troller may have as many as four poles, two main poles and two smaller ones toward the bow. With experience, the whole procedure may take only 30 minutes.

When a fish is hooked, the process is reversed and each spread must be taken in until the spread with the catch may be brought aboard. If a line has 18 spreads rigged and one fish happens to take the bottom spread, the fisherman must haul in all 18 spreads and unclip them to get to the one fish. It can be hard, frustrating work—particularly if that bottom spread is taken by a halibut out of season.

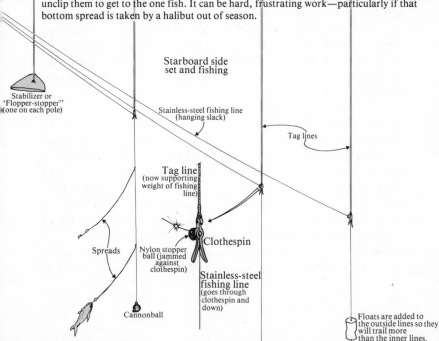

Spring line

Starboard side
set and fishing

Stabilizer or
'Flopper-stopper"
(one on each pole)

Stainless-steel fishing line
(hanging slack)

Tag lines

Tag line
(now supporting
weight of fishing
line)

Clothespin

Spreads

Nylon stopper
ball (jammed
against
clothespin)

Stainless-steel
fishing line
(goes through
clothespin and
down)

Cannonball

Floats are added to
the outside lines so they
will trail more
than the inner lines.

the cockpit, something big breaks water 100 yards behind the boat. A sea lion! He tosses something silvery into the air—my salmon.

I run inside for my rifle, shouting, "You damn critter!" I wait for him to surface again. He can't eat underwater, he must come up and toss the fish into the air to tear out a chunk, then catch it as it comes down.

He surfaces almost out of rifle range. I shoot half-heartedly and miss by a long ways because of the roll of the boat. Angrily I haul up the line. A leader is broken and a flasher missing. I replace them and rebait.

I wonder if he will follow me. A sea lion will often tag along just out of rifle shot, diving every few minutes to check the gear. If there's anything there he wants, he'll take it. Big red kings are his favorite. My lunch is cold.

About 1 P.M. a brisk, cold northerly wind springs up and within moments a small sea and whitecaps are running. The thermometer is down to 38°F. A cloud passes across Veta Bay and a few flakes of snow fall. The trolling hatches of other boats are empty also. I look longingly toward Chirikof Bay, sheltered from the wind.

I console myself with thoughts of warm summer days ahead . . . days when many fish will bite. I open a dog-eared, out-of-date copy of *Reader's Digest* and begin to read. The article becomes more interesting. The next time I look up, a large ball of kelp, seaweed and logs, all wound together, is directly ahead. The magazine falls to the deck as I release the automatic pilot and spin the wheel hard.

I'm too late. The mass catches on the stabilizer, splits in half and straddles the inside trolling line. Coatless, I rush back and shove in on the gurdie to take the strain off the wire. Too late again, the tag line parts and goes flying in the wind. The boat is in a hard turn and the tip line also becomes fouled in the mess; the tip tag line breaks. Now both lines and leads are hanging side by side on the trolling blocks. I'll have to haul them up together to keep the leaders from tangling and breaking off. An hour later I have them all untangled and back in the water again.

Now the sea is rough enough to cause the boat to lurch badly. It goes up and down in the southwest swell, with a northerly sea on

The frigid work of glazing salmon at -20° F in the hold of the Donna C. *The hold is refrigerated so the fish need not be packed in ice.*

top. I've been operating 9½ hours. Counting lost gear and fuel, I'm $10 in the red so far today. I settle down for what promises to be a long, boring afternoon.

About 4 P.M. the wind dies suddenly. I'm halfway between Cape Addington and Granite Point. Spotting bird activity ahead, I change course. It's the kittiwakes. They've been offshore and now are working their way into Veta Bay. They're diving and wheeling in regimented unison. Occasionally, a bird dives to his wing joints in the clear, green sea and comes up gobbling tiny

At the fish-buyer's dock, Dale Caldwell fills the unloading bucket with king salmon in the hold of the Laverne II. *On this boat there was no refrigeration, so the catch had to be iced.*

opossum shrimp. I circle the flock several times, admire their sporty lines and hope there is a salmon lurking under the shrimp.

I see two boats running toward Cone Island. Evidently others are having a hard time catching fish and have decided to give up. As I don my coat and start for the stern to pull in the gear, I hear one short sentence from the speaker above my head.

"Over this way, Frank." I recognize Bob Gay's voice. I look around for the *Suzie M.* Through the glasses I make out the silhouette, almost on the "twelve," a jagged 12-fathom reef in the center of the bay. The twelve is laced with trolling wire and lead, but between the reef and Outer Point is a good 30-fathom drag. I shorten up to 26 fathoms and head toward the *Suzie M.*

As I near the boat, Bob is on the bow waving and pointing. He has 13 fish. I burn with envy. I run my gear and shake off several bass and chicken halibut. The *Suzie M* is turning and wheeling all over the area. It's nearly the same spot where I debated setting out my gear this morning.

The sea is almost flat and a warm sun comes out from behind the clouds. It's springlike, actually pleasant to be on deck. I cut fancy figure eights, change my speed, the depth of my gear and the gear itself. More boats pass by on their way to harbor. I turn up the stove and put spuds in the oven. I've been operating 12 hours without catching a single salmon.

Back in the trolling hatch I watch the tips of my poles hopefully. Then I start to bait with herring. When I look up, both poles are shaking. Fish! Then I remember I'm in a danger zone. I look at the fathometer and find I've forgotten to switch from the one up forward. Quickly I run inside and read 20 fathoms. I open the throttle wide. The diesel rumbles and the poles stop shaking as the momentum lifts the leads off the bottom. The meter now shows 18. I spin the wheel toward what I hope is deeper water. The boat is now going full speed. I keep my eyes on the meter; 19, 20, 24, then suddenly 28 and 30. Ah, I'm back in safe depths. The fathometer is a wonderful instrument that has had a tremendous impact on trolling. When trolling around pinnacles and reefs, it can save thousands of dollars' worth of gear.

I ease back on the throttle and look around to check my bearings—a cliffy hillside over by Kelly Cove and the whitish Granite Point. I'm still outside of safe ground! I point the bow inshore and charge madly, the wires hanging high out of the water.

Again the heavy leads begin to jerk. The meter says 15. I have 26 fathoms of wire out. What am I doing in here? I shove the throttle wide open and cringe, expecting broken rigging to crash down any moment. The port bow line gives a mighty jerk and goes slack. Damn! I've lost a 50-pounder.

Suddenly I'm in 32 fathoms, soft bottom. I slow down and examine what's left of the gear. The port bow line has broken below the top leader. The lead, three spreads and the expensive rubber snubbers are gone. The tag line is broken, dangling in the breeze.

The starboard bow yields a 30-pound king on the top leader. The salmon is soon quivering on deck, disgorging long, green needlefish. The salmon won't pay for the lost gear but he's a morale booster. The second leader holds another one. The bottom two leaders produce one small halibut and a gray cod that I release. The halibut lunges for the bottom and the cod floats helplessly with its air sac distended.

The first main line is empty except for the bottom hook, which somehow managed to snag a starfish. That's dredging bottom! The other main is loaded, two gray cod and two salmon. All four lines are now aboard. This would be the time to quit. But it's a nice evening. Off toward Chirikof I see several boats still working. Reluctantly I put the gear out again. There's fish to clean and I have to repair the broken line and put on a new lead for the morning. I set the gear out to 30 fathoms. From the ton of lead in the stern I select a 50-pounder and fasten it to the broken wire.

I place one of the fish on its back on the cleaning trough and reach for the knife. Over my head a dozen sea gulls gather, screaming with delight. They circle frantically while I cut out the gills, slit the belly and twist the insides free. I hurl the whole bloody mess as far as I can. With ecstatic squeals, the gulls dive in unison and begin gobbling. Other gulls see the action and hurry over. They're too late. Screaming their indignation they swoop around the stern, waiting their chance for an evening snack.

I put another salmon into the trough. After removing the insides I slit the stomach open. About a hundred needlefish tumble out onto the deck. The gulls are ready. When I fling the insides they all plunge so vigorously into the mess they spoil each other's aim. Most of the insides are forced underwater. Some of the wiser birds leap into the air, dive headlong into the water up to their backs, grasp the offal and bring it to the surface, but they are too winded to take a bite. Into this fracas I hurl the tasty needlefish. All noise stops; the birds are too busy gobbling to waste their breath screaming. By the time the third pile of entrails is consumed, the birds have forgotten their differences and are as chummy as ever.

"With ecstatic squeals, the gulls dive in unison and begin gobbling."

It's time to get dinner. The spuds are ready. I dip two dozen small cubes of halibut in batter and place them in the smoking skillet. The grease foams up and turns them golden brown. I enjoy a splendid evening meal. Dinner over, I drink cups of scalding tea and listen to the news from station KTKN in Ketchikan. The news, as usual, is bad. The world may collapse before dawn. I shut off the radio in disgust.

By the time I finish the dishes, jump into the hold and ice my four fish, we're off Granite Point. The snow-covered peaks of Baker Island cast heroic shadows onto tranquil Veta Bay. One troller is still visible, the others have mysteriously disappeared.

I turn to Channel 21 on the CB. "Is that you, Red?"

"Yeah, you bet. Are you catching anything up there?"

"No, nothing," I say. "Looks like we're in for another good night's sleep. Do you think you can sleep without the anchor chain rattling and the wind huffing and puffing?"

"I can always sleep. That's all I've wanted to do all day."

"I know what you mean. It's been a slow go for me. I suppose you really slugged 'em? Getting an early start and all . . . ?"

Red's infectious laugh lifts the weight off my shoulders and reminds me that the world isn't ending just because I had a poor day.

"About one more day like today and I'm going to be steaming west," Red says, "toward that island over there."

I know what he means. We both often move toward Sitka about this time of year. "Did you get the word?" I ask.

"No. But the fishing can't be any worse. At least there's a movie in Sitka."

"There's a movie in Craig, once a week."

"I've got to stay out of there," he says laughing. "Last time I was in, the pool sharks took me for a dollar. On this kind of fishing I can't afford losses like that."

"You could always call Ila and have her sell some chinchillas."
I often tease Red about his chinchillas, a venture in its infancy with all the money so far going out.

I hear him yawn. "I can always borrow from Edmund," he answers. "He's had a flock of sea gulls around his stern again all day."

"Yeah, I'm going to stay out until all you highliners go in.

After that, maybe I can catch a fish. You guys have the salmon so confused with all the fancy gear you're dragging that I haven't been able to get them to bite today."

"Don't feel alone," Red says. "I'm going to haul the gear and find me a hide-e-hole for the night. See you in the harbor."

"Good night, Red. I hope you have a couple of big ones on the gear."

The bay behind Cape Chirikof is open only to the southwest. It's boxed in on the other three sides by steep cliffs and mountains. The bottom shoals gradually at the head and there's a nice white sand beach with piles of drift on it. I'll anchor there.

The gear is aboard now and I'm running full speed. I pass between the cape and the small, rocky, barren island just inside the bay. Off to my port side the swells break heavily against sheer cliffs, causing blankets of white foam to gather on the surface.

Six boats are anchored with their poles down and stabilizers out; the *Tuckahoe*; *High C*; *Sharyn A*; *Tacora*, with Roy Dinwitti of Seattle; *Kruzof*, captained by owner Ray Northrup of Sitka; and the *Argo* with Herb Bromley of Port Townsend. There's an anchorage between the *Tuckahoe* and the *Argo* in 7 fathoms. Twenty fathoms of chain follow the anchor to the bottom.

What a relief to shut off the diesel. The silence washes over me like a soothing balm. Thank goodness there's nothing to do but put on the anchor light and hit the sack. I peek at my watch as I turn out the light. It's 9 P.M. I have 7 hours before daylight. Then I'll arise, start the engine, pump the bilge, put the coffee on and begin all over again. The search for salmon will resume, day after day after day—until spring gives way to the short, northern summer and the summer turns to fall.

Lapp Sam

During the 1940's, chinook salmon swarmed around Southeastern Alaska in vast schools. Port Alexander, now an almost deserted fishing village on the southern tip of Baranof Island, was then a thriving port, complete with processors, cafes, machine shops, bars, a library and a red-light district. Many were the stories I heard from old-timers.

Sam Anderson was one of them, a commercial fisherman to the core. He was born in Lapland some 70 years before I first met him, which accounted for his nickname, Lapp Sam. He went to sea at the age of 14 and was baptized in the rigorous fisherman's life in the icy waters off North Cape, Norway, where cod was king. When Sam was in his twenties he migrated to Alaska and for years he lived in Port Alexander. He claimed a person could walk the full length of the harbor on Sundays, a day on which all fishing was closed, without ever leaving the decks of the boats tied up and anchored there.

In those days salmon trolling was done by hand. The boats were less than 18 feet in length and rigged with oars and sail. Troll lines were cotton and the leads were pulled aboard by hand. It was a hard, dangerous life. Living in tents near the fishing grounds or under tarps thrown across the bow, a hand troller had to be mighty tough to survive the vile Southeastern climate. Getting started required a minimum amount of capital, and the men were fiercely independent. Sam bought a 14-foot skiff and was soon a highliner, the first out fishing in the morning and the last to row up to the buying scow at night.

Gas engines were heavy, cantankerous and inefficient. Nevertheless, someone installed an engine in a small boat and it was an instant success. An engine to propel the boat left both hands free to pull the gear. Boats soon became larger. Before World War I a 30-footer with a 9-horsepower Frisco Standard was a big troller. (Today's large trollers are 60-footers powered by 250-horsepower diesels.)

Catching a boatload of king salmon was usually easy during the early days. Selling them was the difficulty. Red-fleshed kings sometimes brought as little as 3 cents a pound. The white-fleshed kings were either tossed back or kept for personal use; the buyers refused to accept them. Although there is no difference in taste or quality, even today the whites are lower priced.

The gasoline engine was only the first step in the modernization of the hand-troller fleet. It wasn't long until someone managed to rig a system of belts and pulleys from the engine to a spool, or gurdie. Instead of cotton line, the gurdies were filled with stainless steel wire and heavier leads could be used.

Sam was one of the first to recognize the importance of power. While many of his fellow hand trollers scoffed at such fancy equipment, Sam ordered a power troller. He also gill-netted for salmon, but his preference was trolling—always on a small boat he could handle easily by himself.

The king salmon that swarmed around Cape Ommaney were mostly of Columbia River origin. When that great salmon-producing river became choked with dams, the runs around Port Alexander deteriorated and the town withered and died. However, a workable herring fishery still existed. Sam said some mornings he counted as many as 14 large herring seiners rounding the cape from their fishing areas in Larch Bay on their way up Chatham Strait to the refineries at Port Armstrong, Port Walter and Little Port Walter.

A few trollers stayed on. Bert Olson, Syvert Hansen and Sam were certain the salmon runs would return. But after a few years with the salmon still scarce, Sam abandoned the comfortable three-room house on the back bay and migrated down the coast looking for a new location. Southeastern Alaska's infamous weather soon began to reclaim the homes in Port Alexander. Rain and snow found their way through the untended roofs. Doors were blown ajar by gales. The luxurious plant growth, common throughout the Alexander Archipelago, engulfed everything—houses, pathways and woodsheds.

Sam and his wife didn't stop until they reached California's Humbolt Bay. Salmon fishing wasn't the best there either, but World War II was on and the price of albacore was almost $700 a ton. Sam began trolling. Meanwhile, his wife became interested in real estate.

When Sam's wife died unexpectedly he found himself owner of considerable property—none of which he cared a whit about. Sad and lonely, he loaded his few personal possessions aboard his boat and worked his way back up the coast. The war was over, fish prices were low and Sam longed for his old stomping grounds in Alaska.

Two years after leaving California, Sam tied up to the float in Port Alexander. The harbor was deserted. Salmonberries and devil's club surrounded his house. With a machete he chopped a trail along the old familiar pathway. Few things in the house had been disturbed.

A few years later I met Lapp Sam. At the time I was hand-trolling with a small boat. The cabin was so tiny I barely had room in which to stretch out for a few hours' rest. During periods of bad weather, living in that cramped, damp space was miserable. Perhaps remembering his days of hand-trolling and living in a tent, Sam offered me the use of his house.

Lapp Sam was small and wiry, with that tough, rawboned look so common to arctic people who for centuries have been accustomed to rigorous outdoor living. For half a century this little man had survived bitter wind, numbing cold rain and the glare of the sun while working on a pitching deck.

His pale gray eyes, surrounded by a sea of leathery wrinkles, were unusually bright and keen. His hands were misshapen, his

The fishing village of Port Alexander, Alaska, at its heyday in 1935. The large building in the center at the water's edge is the town library. Lapp Sam's house, hidden in this photo, was on the other side of the narrow isthmus.

fingers twisted and his knuckles enlarged from endlessly working in icy water with nets and lines. A crop of wild gray hair twisted every which way, as if perpetually whipped by sea winds. It was generally uncombed, in need of a trim and protruding from a battered black woolen seaman's cap.

Sam's clothing varied little except with two seasons. Summer found him in surplus army togs. All winter he was bundled up in woolen underwear, heavy woolen fishermen's pants and stag shirt. He was especially fond of an old hand-knit Cowichan sweater, which at one time probably had been white. This sweater was invariably worn underneath his oilskin coat on the many blustery days encountered on the salmon grounds. Like most northern seafaring men, Sam was reluctant to substitute any new material for wool. (And rightly so; only wool will retain warmth when wet.)

Lapp Sam wore heavy rubber hip boots rain or shine. These boots were rolled down below the knees except when he was in

37

oilskins, then they were extended full length underneath. In his heavy woolens, stiff oilskins and clumsy hip boots, how this little fellow clambered around the docks, or boarded his vessel and managed to work long 16-hour days on a heaving, slimy deck is a wonder.

Around the house, Sam wore a pair of sheepskin-lined slippers that he'd found in a surplus store. He once showed me a "new" suit—purchased at a Seattle Salvation Army store.

Lapp Sam lived and worked quietly. He didn't smoke, chew or drink. His manner was reserved and sometimes cynical, especially of anyone in authority. His voice was thin, with a hint of a Nordic accent but different from the typical Norwegian-American accent.

Although Lapp Sam had plenty of money he lived an unbelievably frugal life. His food supply—for an outpost like Port Alexander where people normally stocked heavily—was sparse. A trip into his storeroom would have struck chills in the heart of a hardened relief worker. Even though the nearest grocery store was in Sitka, 65 miles away by boat, his shelves contained only a bit of flour, sugar, salt and canned milk, a few potatoes, onions, some oatmeal and raisins. Sam always bought coffee in quantity, though, and cases of Melba toast.

His main food was fish, especially halibut and lingcod. Like most people who depend on fish for their source of protein, Sam preferred it either baked or boiled—never fried. His favorite dish (which I couldn't stand) was halibut and spuds boiled together. Perhaps it was his diet, combined with outdoor living, that was responsible for the remarkable health he enjoyed.

Sam's weather-forecasting abilities were extraordinary. Although he didn't own a radio he usually knew when it was going to blow. His only instrument was a barometer and he watched it carefully, tapping the glass lightly with his finger and resetting the pointer religiously. If the sun were shining, Sam would study the clouds carefully before untying his boat. Many a time when I observed Sam's boat coming in early, a late afternoon blow sprang up and caught most of the others off the cape.

Lapp Sam's vessel was a 32-foot, transom-stern, combination troller/gill-netter. If anyone admired anything about his boat, which didn't have a name, only a number, Sam was quick to point out that the vessel was built in Astoria, Oregon, by Finnish boatbuilders. The way he said this left little doubt that the Finns were the only people who possessed the necessary skills and patience to fashion a really good boat from wood. One might name a dozen faults about a boat—it might be a roller, wet in the stern, or steer badly in a following sea—but if the boat was built by Finns, to Sam's way of thinking it was a good boat.

Sam had survived several close shaves with Davy Jones's locker. I managed to get him talking about some of his experiences during a stormy evening while the wind howled and rain beat against the windows of the old house.

One winter during the 1930's Sam had urgent business to tend to in Ketchikan. At the time he owned a 30-foot Columbia River boat powered by a 9-horsepower Frisco Standard. For days he watched the weather, waiting for a break in the continuous gales that seem to sweep the area around Port Alexander during the winter.

The first leg of his voyage would be 20 miles of open water, across the entrance to Chatham Strait between Cape Ommaney and Cape Decision. Chatham Strait can be a very bad stretch of water because of its strong tides. The only mechanical equipment Sam had on his boat was an engine. His only navigational equipment was a compass. For light he used a coal-oil lantern.

Finally the storm let up and Sam started on the 4-hour crossing. When he was about two-thirds of the way across, the gale resumed. Heavy snow cut visibility to zero. The wind was blowing about 50 knots and darkness descended an hour before the usual 4 P.M. Thoroughly lost, Sam held a course he hoped would take him safely across the strait to round Cape Decision at the southern tip of Kuiu Island. Although he knew of several harbors nearby, he did not intend to approach land in the blinding snow.

Then, above the howl of the gale, a new sound reached his ears. He opened the pilothouse door and stepped outside. The sound was unmistakable—the booming of breakers smashing against solid rock. Because he was close to Kuiu Island, Sam assumed he was approaching that shoreline. He swung the wheel, pointed the bow southwest and opened the throttle wide. Snow covered the windows. When he opened one window in order to see, water came through in spurts that soon would have sunk the boat.

The fish docks at Port Alexander, 1935. There was a fish processing plant near the spot from which this photo was taken.

Ordway photo, courtesy of Dick Gore

Suddenly he felt the boat lift high into the air. Then came a sickening dive, almost straight down. The windows burst inward with a shower of glass. The engine died.

"I lost track of what happened after that," Sam related. "The next thing I remember, I was lying across my swamped skiff, my arms locked around the seat. I could hear the breakers boiling only a few yards away. There was no sign of my boat."

Sam felt around under the icy water and found the bailing can lashed to its line. His fingers also grasped the oars, lashed across the seat as his father had taught him to do during his codfishing days. He began bailing like mad. By the time he got most of the water out of the skiff, he could no longer hear the breakers.

"That was encouraging," Sam said. "If what I thought was the Kuiu shore was only an offshore rock, I had a chance to row to safety yet."

He got the oars working and rowed slowly before the seas with the wind on his right cheek. About midnight the snow stopped. When he could see the snow-covered mountaintops, he knew where he was and what had sunk his boat. He'd been on Crowley Breaker, a dangerous underwater rock a mile or so off Point Crowley. He evidently had come upon the breaker from the inside, and when he changed course to escape, he steered straight onto the rock.

After getting his bearings he set a course for Table Bay. A few days later he walked in on the lighthouse keepers at Cape Decision. Within a week he had flagged a passing boat and was in Ketchikan looking for another troller.

About every 20 years a storm, which would be named if it were on the populated East Coast, strikes the Pacific Northwest. One such windstorm hit the area around Coronation Island, where many tragedies have occurred. Early in the century the *Star of Bengal* was driven ashore at Helm Point on Coronation with a terrible loss of life. The island has a bad reputation for williwaws. It is a spooky place and not one I'd choose to weather a blow.

During the thirties Sam and other trollers were anchored behind the island when the williwaws began. Many boats broke anchor and were driven ashore. It was a case of every man for himself, because in winds of 100 knots, no boat can do much to help another.

Sam's troller was simply laid over on her side until she filled with water. Sam kicked off his heavy boots, jumped overboard and swam for shore. When he reached the beach, the undertow was so strong he couldn't gain the safety of high ground.

He was hanging net in the shed the day he related this story. Laying the net needle aside, he rolled up his sleeves and showed me ugly scars on his elbows and forearms.

"The only way I could get ashore was to dive to the bottom and hang onto the rocks while the surge went out. Barnacles did this to my arms."

Lapp Sam finally made his way above the crashing waves and then lost consciousness. When he came to, he saw a troller named Garrison standing over him.

Garrison, long-time owner of the *Norma*, also lost his boat that day but had managed to get ashore safely. He was walking along the beach when he discovered what he thought was a corpse. He went to drag it away from the tide but as he bent over the body, the man sat up and began to vomit sea water.

Sam was emphatic that only wood or coal were fit fuels to heat a home or a boat. He was so fond of the wood-burning heater he had in his house in Port Alexander, that he even talked to it. The stove was low and flat on top, with ample room for cooking on its surface. Two-foot chunks of wood went in through a front door.

Years ago the fishing fleet converted their stoves to oil, because chopping wood and keeping coal on a small boat was a lot of trouble. Sam finally decided to follow suit, but claimed he hated that newfangled potburner right from the start. Within a few weeks the stove quit.

"Every time I went into the cold fo'c'sle and saw that stove I'd get mad again," he said. "For a couple days I got by. Fishing was good and I hated to quit. By wiring cans of food to the engine exhaust I managed to last, but having no hot coffee was more'n I could take."

"What'd you do?" I asked.

"The only sensible thing. I ripped out the copper tubing and smashed the pot and hurled the whole thing overboard. Then I pulled the gear and headed for Soakum Pete's marine store in Sitka where I could get some coal grates."

Sam leaned back laughing. "Since then I've never missed having hot coffee."

Lapp Sam's clothing and bedding, as well as his face and hands, were usually dark from coal dust when he was living on his boat. The sound of his ax chopping kindling on deck awakened many a harbor mate.

In the late fall the gill-net fleet moved into Lynn Canal to catch the silvers and chums on their way to the Chilkat River. Lapp Sam's stovepipe belching clouds of black smoke and sparks served the other fishermen well as a landmark. They knew Sam had a nose for finding fish, and they came close to set their nets.

Several seasons passed without my seeing Lapp Sam. Meanwhile I'd heard that he had moved to Meyers Chuck, a community of trollers 35 miles north of Ketchikan.

One wet blustery fall day while I was homeward bound between Sitka and Ketchikan, I stopped at Meyers Chuck. Lapp Sam's familiar old gray boat was tied to the float. Lonesome Pete told me how to reach Sam's cabin on the back chuck. I took the rowboat.

Spring means bottom painting. The pride of the fleet in Port Alexander, about 1935. The masts stepped on the foredeck to support the bow poles have not been used on trollers for 30 years now.

The cabin was perched above the high-tide line on a steep and rocky shore. Jet-black ravens watched suspiciously as I tied the skiff and climbed the beach. Fragrant spruce smoke spiraled upward from a blackened stovepipe protruding at a rakish angle from the cabin's shake roof.

Lapp Sam opened the door. He still wore the same woolen army clothes he had worn when I saw him last. His shoulders were more stooped, his fingers stiffer and his hair grayer but his eyes were as bright and keen as ever.

"Come in, come in," he cackled happily, "and see your old friend from Port Alexander."

"Old friend?" I wondered who that could be. I politely scraped my boots, although I don't know why, as the floor was littered with scraps of wood. A homemade table and a few chairs occupied the center of the room, and several old sea chests lined the walls. In one corner sat Sam's beloved cast-iron heater. Its warmth felt good on the chill fall day. I walked to the stove and held my hands over its top.

"You 'member her then?" Sam laughed. "She's as good as new. They don't make stoves like that nowadays, do they?"

So this was the old friend.

"How come you left that nice three-room house in Alexander?" I asked.

"Ack!" Sam spat, missing the slop bucket by several inches. "That blow hole. All winter long the wind goes woo, wooo, woooooo. I got sick of it. Couldn't get out fishing. Besides," he looked at me sideways, "I got this." He rummaged through a drawer in one of the chests, then produced a slip of paper.

I held it to the window. "A tax bill. I got one, too, and so did everyone else. We're a state now."

"A state, sure. But no politician ever lifted a finger in Alexander. Before you get paid you gotta do something! Who put in the water system? Who built the sidewalks? The townspeople. The state never did a thing for us nor the territory either. I told 'em where they could put this bill. Thirty-eight dollars—for what?"

"So you left."

"I picked up my stove and my rocking chair and took off."

"Now you'll pay taxes here."

"No way. This place is on government land." Sam whispered. "Guess how much I paid?"

I shook my head.

"Two hundred and fifty dollars—and the woodshed is full of dry spruce." Sam cackled with glee.

"You made a steal. Now, do you want to see my boat?"

"You bought a boat?"

"Two years ago. A 42-footer, the *Laverne II*."

"Is it Finn-built?"

"Nope. Native. Andrew Hope from Sitka. Know him?"

"Sure. Good boatbuilder. Not like the Finns, but a good man." He reached for the Cowichan sweater. He must have noticed me staring at it. The garment was almost black now, except the collar which was smeared with copper paint. "One thing the Finns can't do as well as the Indians is make these sweaters," Sam added. "I bought this one 20 years ago in Cowichan Bay and it's still as good as new."

Sam's old eyes flew as he examined my boat's rigging, the Kolstrand gurdies and the anchor gear. He was quiet until we entered the galley and he saw the Olympic stove. He walked over and lifted the lid, then turned and looked at me reproachfully. "An oil burner! Well, you'll soon have that thing out of there. Put in some wood grates. Then you'll have a home fit for a king."

Sam continued on his inspection trip. He grunted when he discovered my automatic pilot was a Freeman. In the engine room he patted the new Jimmy diesel. "These Jimmys are good, but the Volvo Penta's better. That Penta is as dependable as death and taxes," said Lapp Sam.

He sat down in the galley and asked me all about the new herring hookups and which spoons had produced that season. Then he startled me by announcing that he was taking a trip to Eureka. He'd heard that the salmon were returning to the northern California coast.

I didn't believe him. He was about 75. But sure enough, a few weeks later his old boat showed up alongside mine in Thomas Basin. He asked me to keep her pumped while he was gone to Eureka. "It won't be no trouble," he added. "She's Finn-built, you know."

Two months later he was back, full of enthusiasm for the new venture. He wore a "new" suit and black hat, stylish 30 years earlier. I insisted he come to dinner. I also was becoming alarmed with statehood and taxes, so this time it was my turn to pump him. I finally talked him into showing me some new herring hooks he'd found in California.

"It's true," he said, "the fish are back. I'm leaving as soon as I get a new motor in the boat and my junk from the Chuck."

I helped him take the old motor out, but when the new one arrived it wasn't exactly what he had ordered. Sam refused to take delivery and had the engine sent back. He reinstalled the old engine and returned to Meyers Chuck.

I didn't see much of Lapp Sam after that. Each spring I worked the great Alaskan capes—Felix, Bartolome, Addington,

Port Alexander's bustling days are now past, the houses empty. The Laverne II *(left) shares the pier with the* Genador *and the* Kingfish.

Ommaney, Edgecumbe, Cross and Fairweather. I watched for Sam along the outside coast, although I knew that if he were still fishing he'd more likely be taking it easy somewhere inside where the water was smoother.

It wasn't until April 1969 that my wife, Donna, and I stopped off in Meyers Chuck en route between Ketchikan and Pelican, and learned that Lapp Sam had found his final snug harbor in Hoquiam, Washington, exact date of death unknown.

In June I made it a point to stop in Port Alexander. The harbor was alive with birds and the Sitka spruce and cedar along the water's edge was as beautiful as ever. We fought our way through the briars and brush to Sam's old house. The stained-glass window in the front door had been stolen. Someone had built an open fire in the living room near where Sam's old cast-iron stove had stood. Deer tracks dimpled the sand at his back door. The beach was ablaze with Indian paintbrush.

We then hiked the trail to the inner harbor. It was a sunny day and, as I expected, we found elderly Syvert Hansen working on his well-kept lawn.

I asked Hansen if he knew Lapp Sam Anderson was dead.

The old man sat down on a bench and mopped the sweat from his face. "No," he said softly. "Sam Anderson—dead! I didn't tink it vas possible."

"Why do you say that? He was an old man."

"I know. I've known Lapp Sam for more years dan I care to remember. But I alvays tought he vas too tough to die."

After talking about the old days for a few minutes, we left Hansen sitting, reminiscing in his neat yard. We wanted to make Sitka before dark. At Cape Ommaney the sea seethed and rumbled restlessly but remained reasonably calm, and three hours later we were off Redfish Cape.

Just inside was one of Sam's favorite anchorages. He'd spent many nights in Tenfathom Anchorage, cleaning salmon by the light of a coal-oil lantern. Now no trollers were in sight. A little farther up was Snipe Bay. Once several packers a day loaded up in Snipe from the trollers, but we saw only one boat working off the bay. It would take a single packer all season to load up in Snipe Bay now.

We took the shortcut through Cameron Pass and past Goddard Hot Springs into Sitka Sound. Although it was June, the best time of year for trolling this area, we didn't see another troller until we got to Biorka Island.

"You know," I said to Donna as we tied up to the float in Sitka, "it isn't only the old-timers that are about gone. The salmon aren't going to last much longer, either."

A month later we were working off Cape Fairweather. We heard on the marine band that Syvert Hansen had died. The Port Alexander of old is truly no more.

Radio Talk

Although he usually operates in a fleet, a commercial fisherman is isolated without his radio. The quiet operation of gasoline engines in the early days permitted talk between two vessels while they were trolling side by side. The sharp bark of diesel exhausts changed that. Communication is reduced to either hand signals or the radiotelephone. There are only a few frequencies the fisherman can use on the marine band, where congestion is unbelievable. It is like hearing three radios tuned to different broadcast stations, blasting away simultaneously. In order to talk to another vessel, even one only a few miles away, you have to have plenty of power to override other transmitters. Nevertheless, a transmitter is top-priority equipment. Failure of radio equipment at sea can cost an unbelievable amount of lost time and money. In case of sudden fire or engine breakdown on a dangerous lee shore, the radio becomes the thin thread between life and death. Malfunction usually sends the fisherman off for town, which may be several hours' or days' running time away. No matter, the equipment must be fixed and few fishermen have any idea how to make the repairs.

Then along came the citizen's band (CB) radio. This diminutive radio filled a need and was quickly accepted by the fleet. Because of its size, erratic behavior and astonishingly uncertain transmitting range, CB radios were given two nicknames: "Mickey Mouse" and "spook set." Both stuck. Under certain conditions, called "skip," CB signals may be audible for hundreds of miles. The CB is completely unreliable at these long distances, however. But a sleepy troller can be awakened by a caller in Tulsa, Oklahoma, or a farmer talking between his house and barn in Moose Jaw, Saskatchewan, as he begins milking.

By 1960 few trollers lacked CB radios. All close-range traffic was soon on CB, which helped relieve the congestion on the regular marine band. Skippers who would never dream of talking on the marine band about important fishing information, such as the type of spoon the salmon were striking or the depth they were trolling, would do so on CB because they knew what they said rarely traveled more than 20 miles. Fishermen were quick to decide that if lots of good fishing information could be heard on one CB, twice as much might be learned by listening to two at a time. I've known captains who boasted they could listen to the regular marine band, a broadcast band and three CB's simultaneously.

CB's are also put to other uses. Dangerous situations sometimes develop at night while trollers sleep. A boat may begin to drift, putting it on a collision course with another. An anchor may drag, allowing a vessel to move downwind and endanger the boat behind it. Or a steamer might approach in heavy fog. To help avert such sleep-disturbing occurrences, many trollers leave their CB sets on all night.

The following conversation took place over CB radio off the central Oregon coast:

"Jake! Jake, wake up—dammit. There's a log dead ahead of you!"

Silence.

"Jake. Jake, for Pete's sake wake up. [He whistles.] Jake, hit the deck, man, or you're gonna crunch a log."

Silence.

"Jake! Jake! Jake! One-two, one-two, one-two! Oh, Jake! Change course, Cap'n—fast!"

"Whew! You barely missed it, Cap'n. You're a lucky man. Couldn't have been more'n 6 inches from your bow. O.K., buddy boy, sleep away. You're clear now."

I could visualize the situation. Two boats, probably each with only the captain on board, were running together, perhaps en route from the northern albacore grounds off the Oregon-Washington coasts to the Southern California fishery. They were no doubt quite a ways offshore, planning to run all night, and were taking turns napping. One would keep watch while the other depended upon his automatic pilot to keep the course. If a ship or another boat appeared, the CB was used to jar the sleeper from his nap until the danger passed. A simple and seemingly foolproof plan. But where was Jake when he almost hit that log? Had the static of his spook set been keeping him awake, so that in his sleepy stupor he had turned it off? Or was he down in the engine room checking the equipment? I'll never know.

Most fishermen stand by on 2638 or 2748 on the marine band. Pure pandemonium prevails over these two channels each morning when the entire fleet is searching for fish. Besides trollers, seiners, halibuters and gill-netters all struggling to get a word in edgewise, there are also tugs with 150-watt sets that are trying to report to their home offices.

A few moments of listening (about all any sane man can stand), might disclose a worried skipper asking someone to please come back and tell him how to adjust a loran set with its picture shifted two inches to the left; a tug trying to get word to the Seattle office that he needs two sacks of spuds and one seaman—not two seamen and one sack of spuds; a distraught and befuddled troller being notified by a friend that today is Wednesday not Tuesday, and that his enraged wife, whom he thought was flying to meet him tomorrow, is now stamping up and down the dock threatening to return home; or a cruiser skipper insisting long and loud in an inebriated voice that he is qualified for Coast Guard assistance because his supply of ice is exhausted.

Over the years I've made notes of actual radio conversations that took place up and down the coast from Cape Foulweather to Cape Fairweather. Several skippers in the fleet are avidly listened to because they're interesting, informative and amusing. Obviously they enjoy broadcasting. A characteristic universally admired among fishermen is the ability to keep spirits up in the face of adverse conditions. With the fishing terrible, his wife suing for divorce, the boat payment behind and caught offshore in a bad gale, the fisherman who can get on the radio and wisecrack about his predicament will be admired by his colleagues.

A fisherman's sense of humor is sometimes his defense against boredom. After the usual formalities of call signs and making contact, this conversation took place between two halibut boats operating near Pelican, Alaska:

"How many men do you have with you this year? Four? Same as last? Over."

"No. We always used to have four, but that was back when we played bridge and needed 'em. Nowadays we play cribbage. So we need only two."

In a country where daylight comes at 3 A.M. and darkness at 11 P.M., the fishing often goes on all through the daylight hours, so you can imagine how much card playing takes place. On harbor days there's sleep to catch up on and gear to overhaul. The excuse of a change of card games showed there had been a switch from coil gear to snap-on gear in the face of economic pressures, with the consequent reduction of manpower. New techniques and equipment and rising labor costs have affected fishing, as well as other industries.

Off Cape Addington one spring morning I taped a conversation between two trollers. One had just arrived on the grounds from Seattle, and the other was filling him in on what he'd missed—mostly a storm. After a while the newcomer asked, "I suppose you've got your wife with you again this year?"

"Nope. She stayed home."

"Oh? I hope she's not sick or anything?"

"Nope. She violated Section One of the Master's and Mate's Agreement."

A long silence. "What is that?"

"She's pregnant."

One spring the trollers who generally fish on the Fairweather grounds had been harassed more than usual by a series of southeasters and easterlies that had been striking with the swiftness of a rattlesnake and the savage force of a hurricane. The

Radiotelephone sets festoon the overhead in the pilothouse of the Donna C. *The radio is frequently the fisherman's only contact with society for days on end, and sometimes it is his savior.*

fishermen spent more time peering over their shoulders into the southeast than looking at the tips of their poles. The weather broadcast from Yakutat was listened to with almost religious dedication, but many needless trips were made to the bay because of forecasts of gales that didn't materialize.

One miserable morning at 10 o'clock I was hanging on inside the pilothouse where it was warm. A huge southerly swell rolled under us, slate gray and endless, like an elephant's hide. The poles of nearby boats swung wildly in great arcs as the vessels rode the swells. Two captains began talking on the Mickey Mouse.

"One-two, one-two. Pick me up, Bart? Did you get the Yakutat weather?"

Silence. Bart's boat was alongside and I could see him working in the trolling hatch. He shook two chicken halibut, reset the line, and raced for the warmth of the pilothouse.

"One-two. One-two. Morning, Bart. Pick me up, Bart?"

I knew Bart was in the galley, struggling out of his heavy coat, wiping the herring slime off his numb, red hands with a paper towel and blowing on them, trying to warm them enough so he could grasp the mike and answer.

"Yeah. I'm here. I was out back. Can't you give a man a minute to thaw out his fingers?"

"What were you doing out there?"

"Shaking Ping-Pong paddles, what else?"

I chuckled at his description of the flat halibut.

"Did you get Yakutat?" the other man asked. "Some of the guys are pulling their gear and taking off to the east."

"Yeah. I got it. Southeast, 15 to 25, Spencer to Yakutat. From the looks of the sky, that forecast sounds about right: 15 added to 25 makes about 40. That's what it'll probably blow. Man! I'm getting tired of listening to that same old record. Why doesn't he change to the one he uses when he's on his summer vacation—the one that says 'light to moderate westerlies'?"

"He's saving that for a couple of days in August. I think you've misjudged what he meant by 15 to 25 though. Doesn't that mean the height of the seas?"

(Laughter.) "Either that or else he means from 15 to 25 of us stupid guys are going to get the hell kicked out of us before we get in. Let's pull the junk aboard and get cracking."

In Alaskan waters the good fishing spots are often small in area. For this reason there is much secrecy about the fishing and the use of codes is widespread. Several boats, known as coding partners, usually operate in a group.

This particular conversation took place between two coding partners one day when several newcomers were fishing with the regular group around the rock piles off Shelikof and Gilmer bays on Kruzof Island's outside coast.

"Pick me up, Victor?"

"You bet, Curt. How's it going? Any business yet?"

"Naw. Mighty slow. A red and a green. How about you?" (Red was probably five, and green, one. I figured Curt had six fish for the morning.)

"A red and a green! You're really slugging 'em. I've only caught a lousy purple. What are you catching yours on?" (The "lousy purple" was the code for 20. His idea was to confuse those who might be listening and throw them off the track of where the fishing was the best.)

There was a slight pause as Curt digested this; Victor had almost four times as many fish as he had. "A purple," he finally stammered. "Well, that isn't much, I'll agree, but it's better than nothing. I've been catching my fish on the stuff we made up last time we were in town. Remember?"

"Yeah, I remember. I can't get anything to work for me today. The best I've found is that stuff we bought in Bella Bella on the way south two years ago."

"Oh, yeah? What size hook are you using?"

"Mustad, 95-10. Number 7. Need some?"

"Nope. How deep are you dragging out there, Victor?"

"Twenty-five. There's a 15 in between us somewhere, so look out."

"The chart doesn't show any 15 here!"

"It's there. I've hit it twice now."

"O.K., partner. I'll take your word on it."

Curt's boat pointed straight for his friend, just the opposite of what a newcomer listening in might expect. He went out back and dropped all four lines down to 25 fathoms. His meter blinked out a steady 30 to 35 fathoms as he trolled up and back alongside his partner's boat. Twice he saw Victor run out, haul a line, and fling a big king aboard. That made 22.

Curt dug in his spare spoon bucket and took out several needlefish spoons—the little jewel Victor said he was catching them on. His confidence renewed, he lowered a line with the needlefish spoons, although he'd never yet caught a fish on one of them.

Behind Victor's boat a flock of sea gulls wheeled and dived as Victor cleaned fish, one right after another. When he finished, he threw several buckets of water on deck and hurried inside.

"Doing any good, partner?" he called.

"No. Nothing." Curt said sourly.

"It's orange over here. Really slow."

That probably meant he was up to 25.

"You get that, Cap? I said it's orange over here."

"Yeah! Yeah. I heard you the first time," Curt snarled. "If

you keep on you'll catch up to me yet." He was mad now, but kept up the discipline of the code.

At that moment Curt's bow poles began jerking. Anxious to catch salmon he had forgotten Victor's warning about the pinnacle rocks and hadn't been watching his meter. When he did look, it showed 15 instead of 30.

A cloud of diesel smoke shot skyward from Curt's exhaust as he opened the throttle to get away. Both bow poles bent almost to the water's edge. One broke and hung alongside in the water. The breaking strap on the other let go. The lighter leads on the main poles swung up easily and were saved.

From his pilothouse Victor watched silently.

Another fisherman trolling nearby picked up his mike. "It's a little early to be planting pumpkins, isn't it?"

There was a momentous silence. Another voice joined in, unable to resist the chance to cast his barb into an already aggravated situation. "Maybe Curt doesn't trust banks; puts his cash into lead and deposits it on 'old Matterhorn' there. . . . "

If Curt heard he didn't reply. He was too busy straightening out the mess and spooling on new wire. He finished the day with only three poles and much silence.

Sometimes utter confusion results when messages are relayed by radiotelephone. Vessels in distress, rumors of some imminent catastrophe, or the expectant father situation all offer fertile grounds for verbal mayhem. The following account, although fictitious, is typical of what happens in the world of radiotelephone.

A young fisherman, Joe Dokes, is trolling in Alaskan waters. His pregnant wife is home in Seattle. The day the birth is due is circled on Joe's calendar. He'd like to be there, but with new bills coming up, the best plan is for him to keep his spoons in the water. He has told his wife to contact him by calling the cold storage plant on the land phone. The plant could then contact him on the marine band.

When the pains come a week early, Joe's wife calls her sister-in-law to relay the message to Joe.

"Tell Joe I've gone in early. To contact him, call Frosty Cold Storage at Snowflake, Alaska. Their phone is operated by one of those microwave things so don't be surprised if you have trouble with the call. Tell the cold storage to contact Joe on the *Happy Jack* and inform him that I've gone to the hospital with labor pains. Thanks.''

In an office high above the fish docks of an isolated processing plant in Alaska, the telephone rings.

''Frosty Cold Storage,'' answers the office girl.

As usual, the telephone connection is terrible. She cups her hand over one ear to shut out the roar of the ice-making machinery.

''A message for who? Joe Dokes? The radio operator is out right now but I'll take it. You'll have to speak up though, I can barely . . .''

''Tell him his sister called. His wife is in the hospital with labor pains. I checked with the doctor, though, and he said it might be two more days.''

''Hello, hello. I'm sorry. All I got of that was, tell him his sister called. . . . ''

The voice from Seattle repeats something about pains and two more.

''I think I got it,'' the girl says. She jots down the message: ''Sister called, Joe's wife is in the hospital with pains, might be tumor.''

When the radio operator returns, the girl hands him the message. ''I hope you have better luck over the air than I did,'' she says. ''The reception is sure poor.''

The radioman twirls dials and flips switches on his set. Being a shore station, he isn't allowed to transmit on 2638, the frequency he knows Joe Dokes guards. Instead, he calls on 2566. Failing to get an answer he switches to 2512. When he doesn't rouse anyone there either, he is neither surprised nor discouraged. This is routine.

Note in hand, he goes down the dock, whistling. The *Blackhawk* is there unloading salmon, and its owner, old Edgar, is a good guy—even if he is hard of hearing. He could call the *Happy Jack* and tell Joe the cold storage wanted to talk to him on 2512.

''Sure, be glad to,'' Edgar shouts. ''Always glad to help out a fellow fisherman. But you'll have to wait until I finish unloading.''

"Slippery Joe" Anseln unloads iced fish at Pelican Cold Storage. Pelican, Alaska, is in Lisianski Inlet, just off the Gulf of Alaska near Cape Spencer, some 70 miles south of the Fairweather Ground.

The radioman nods, and goes home for lunch. When he returns, he leans over the railing and shouts down to Edgar, who has finished unloading and is washing down the hold. Water is flying from a pressure hose.

"Edgar. Hey, Edgar. Did you get word to the *Happy Jack*?"

"What'd you say?" Edgar yells, twisting the hose around in an effort to hear above the sound of water. Crushed ice comes down a chute nearby, making a terrible noise. On the other side, a winch whines as it lifts slingloads of halibut from a boat.

Edgar shakes his head. "Can't hear a thing! Shut off that valve by your feet."

"Did you get through?"

"Oh, the call. Yes. I talked to Joe but he doesn't have 2512."

"Would you call him again? Ask if he has 2566."

"Don't have to. Joe wants you to give me the message. I'll call him back on 2638."

"Good idea." The radioman fishes in his pocket for the message. He searches his pants, shirt and coat pockets.

"You didn't lose the message, did you?" Edgar says.

"Oh no. But I must've changed coats while I was home for lunch. However, I remember it was a call from his wife. She said his sister was sick. She's in the hospital with a tumor. He's to call home as soon as he can. Got it?"

Edgar lights a cigarette. "Tell Joe his wife called. Joe's sister is in the hospital and he's supposed to go home as soon as he can."

More ice plunges down the chute and the radioman can't hear Edgar, but he nods.

Out on the fishing grounds, Joe Dokes is waiting for the message to be relayed over 2638. He is sure he knows what it is. The realization that he is probably already a father sinks in slowly. Waiting for confirmation and more information, Joe decides to celebrate. Knowing he would be at sea, he came prepared. Tucked away in the bottom of his sea bag is a bottle. He takes one drink for his new child. The second drink is to his wife's good health. The third is because it is so cold outside.

"Calling the *Happy Jack*. Calling the *Happy Jack*. This is WD 2345, the *Blackhawk*. Do you pick me up out there, Joe?"

"The *Blackhawk*. The *Happy Jack*, WC 9898. Sure Edgar. Over."

"The *Blackhawk* back. Say Joe, I finally got that message. Shall I repeat it now?"

"Yes, Edgar. Go ahead. Is it a boy or girl?"

A pause. Then, "I'm not sure what you mean by that, Joe. But the call was from your wife. She says your sister is in the hospital with stomach cancer. She wants you to fly home right away. Did you get that?"

"Yes, Edgar. Thanks a lot."

"Any return message? I'll make a phone call for you if you want. Anything. . . . ''

Joe thinks for a moment. "That's good of you, Edgar. I can't call home through KOW Seattle, my radio just won't reach, and I'm about 20 hours from town. Would you please have the cold storage send my sister some flowers?"

"It's practically done, Joe. You can count on me. Good luck. *Blackhawk* clear with—I've forgotten the name of your boat."

Joe drops into the trolling hatch and shoves in on a gurdie handle. Nothing happens. He shoves in on another gurdie handle. Nothing happens with that gurdie either. Cursing angrily, Joe goes through the galley and down the ladder into the engine room. He comes back choking and gagging and wiping his eyes on his coat sleeve. "Oil. Hydraulic oil. Must be a broken hose." Joe slows the engine and peers down the hatch again. By now all the oil has spurted out of the broken fitting and the way is clear.

"Damn hose let go," Joe growls to himself. "Well, nothing to do but see if I can fix it. Hope I have enough oil."

"Calling the *Happy Jack*. Calling the *Happy Jack*. This is the *Blackhawk* calling." Again and again the call goes out. Finally Edgar gives up.

"The *Barron* to the *Blackhawk*. Do you receive me, Edgar?"

"The *Blackhawk* back to the *Barron*. You bet I do, Sig. You're coming in loud and clear. Over."

"You're putting out a good signal too, Edgar. The *Happy Jack* is right alongside. I don't know why he doesn't answer. Can I take a message?"

"You sure can, Sig. Tell him there's been a mistake. The radioman got things fouled up. Instead of his sister in the hospital, it's his wife. Can you get that message to him right away, Sig?"

"You bet, Edgar. We'll catch up with him."

Down in the engine room, Joe is working on the broken hose. He's found the extra hose but he can't locate the right fitting. Every few minutes he dashes up to the wheelhouse to peer around to make sure nothing is ahead. Then he goes back to digging through cans and lockers, looking for the fitting. On about the fifth trip to the wheelhouse he sees another boat practically beside him. It is the *Barron*, whose skipper comes on deck and yells, "Channel 2, Joe."

"What'd you say? I can't hear a thing with this exhaust." Joe points to the top of the pilothouse.

The skipper of the *Barron* holds up two fingers on one hand. The other hand he lifts to his mouth in the manner of holding a mike.

Joe understands this right away. He waves, goes inside and turns on his Mickey Mouse.

"Is this thing warmed up yet?" Joe asks.

"Yeah. Barely. Gee, you're a hard guy to get hold of. Edgar tried and tried. Finally I took the call."

"Oh? I've been down in the engine room. I've got a broken hydraulic hose. Can't pull my gear unless I can fix it."

"Is that so. Say, that's too bad. I've got lots of spare parts over here. Be glad to lend you a hand. What is it you need?"

"Hose connector. Female. One-half inch."

"Hmm . . . haven't any of those, I'm sure."

"I think I have one. If I can just find it. What did Edgar want?"

"Oh! The message. Seems the radio operator made a mistake. It's your wife that's in the hospital. Your sister's all right."

Silence.

"Did you get that?"

"Yeah. You say my wife's . . ."

"That's what they said. Hope it's nothing serious. If I can help, let me know. I've gotta go."

"Yeah. Thanks." Joe sinks down on a stool. He wipes his red-rimmed eyes with a greasy hand. Behind the boat, a sea lion lazily tears off another salmon. Joe doesn't move. He sits, staring out the windows. The automatic pilot wheezes and growls as it turns the wooden wheel back and forth. Finally he resumes searching

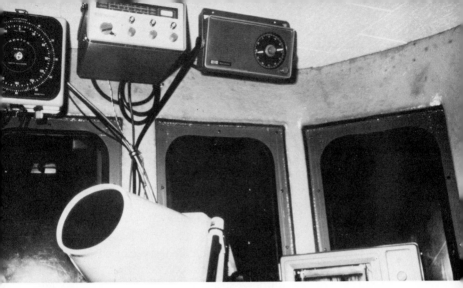

Modern electronics in the pilothouse of the Donna C *include the fathometer, radio, automatic radio direction finder, radar and depth recorder. The boat is also equipped with a loran set for accurate position finding.*

until he finds the fitting. He fixes the break and refills the hydraulic pump with oil. Then he pulls his gear and his stabilizers. A black puff of smoke shoots from his exhaust.

Hours later Joe receives another call. "The *Happy Jack*. Calling the *Happy Jack*. This is the *Blackhawk* calling." Edgar's voice sounds tired.

"The *Happy Jack* back." Joe's voice also sounds drawn.

"Boy, am I glad to get hold of you, Joe. There's another telephone call for you here in town. It just came. Are you listening?"

"Yes. I'm listening."

"This time it was your wife. She said that she's home and everything is O.K. It was just false labor."

"False labor?" Joe looks out the window. The sun is dipping over the horizon. He has had the gear up and has been running toward town for 4 hours. "False labor," he repeats.

"That's what the message said. She's O.K. Did you get that?"

"Roger. I got it fine. She's O.K. Thanks a lot, Edgar."

Joe slows the engine and takes the clutch out of gear. He drops anchor, shuts off the engine and crawls into his bunk. It has been a long, long day in the land of the party line.

Howling with Wolves

"Aowooo. Aowoooo. . . ." The chilling cry carried above the wind's moan through the rigging. A southeast gale ruffled the surface of the harbor. Sheets of cold rain drifted by my pilothouse window, gray ghosts fleeing from the wind.

I jerked awake from an afternoon nap in the pilothouse, stood up, wiped the windows and peered out at the gloomy rain. Only the noise of the rigging, I decided, and lay down again. The wind swirled and whirled in gusts. The boat would creep up over the anchor during a lull, then surge back and fetch up with a neck-snapping, chain-rattling jerk.

Presently, I heard the sound again, much louder this time. "Aowoooooo. Aowoooooo." The eerie cry was followed by a few doglike barks of a timber wolf. Using binoculars, I scanned the beach. The tide was out and the shore was littered with brown rocks and seaweed. There were plenty of places a wolf could hide.

From my helmsman's chair I watched the beach and sipped hot tea. I was anchored in Port San Antonio, Baker Island, a few miles southwest of Craig, Alaska. It was mid March and few trollers were out fishing. For days a mixture of snow and rain, bitter southwest squalls and southeast gales had plagued our efforts. The previous day a southeaster had caught Vince Cameron of *Camelot* and me off Cape Bartolome and sent us scurrying to harbors. The *Camelot* had anchored in Port Santa Cruz, across Bucareli Bay, while I'd gone on into San Antonio so I could fish crab.

Vince and I had voyaged to Alaska together from Port Angeles, Washington, a week earlier. We outfitted in Ketchikan and ran around Cape Chacon to the west coast of Prince of Wales Island. Our destination was the fishing grounds near Craig. The *High C,* owned by Perry Coburn, the *Sharyn A,* with Ed and Ann Allain, and several other boats had been present when we arrived. When the weatherman forecast the southeaster, they decided to cut their trips short and head for home. Home for them was Ketchikan, some 18 hours away.

Vince and I had arrived ahead of the kings. This wasn't the first time it had happened. We were aware of the risks involved in coming north so early and resigned ourselves to waiting.

Something on the beach crossed a patch of light-colored sand. I raised the binoculars. It was a wolf all right, but he was hard to see. I left the snug cabin and ventured out on the wet and windy deck. Again I heard his wild call roll across the harbor. Suddenly I was a small boy again, thrilled by a story I'd read about a boy and his sister. On their way home through a forest, wolves had appeared. The children had taken refuge under an overturned wagon box. I could still remember the terror they experienced as they huddled together under that box while a dozen hungry timber wolves gathered around. I couldn't remember the end of the story.

With binoculars pressed tightly against my eyes, I followed this wolf's movements as he explored the beach. Every few minutes he'd sit, tip back his head and clear his throat by barking, then with his nose up past the vertical, he'd let go with a high-pitched cry. Slowly, in short, wavering jerks, he'd lower his nose. The results were an astonishing range of notes. I laughed. Although the surroundings were certainly different, the manipulations of his vocal cords reminded me of a woman who had sung in our church choir.

After each howl the wolf prowled along the beach, exploring

with his nose. Several times I saw him lift a hind leg and mark what was probably one of his boundary posts. Occasionally he'd turn over boulders the size of a man's head and, with much jaw popping, eat the tiny hermit crabs that tried to escape.

Thoroughly chilled and wet through my shirt, I retreated to the warmth of the galley and sat by the window again. A show like this is one bonus of a troller's lonely life. During some 20 years of knocking around Southeastern, where there are many wolves, this was my first chance to watch one.

Muscle control, I decided. That's how he regulates his voice. Using that technique, I thought I could mimic him. I cleared my throat and tipped my head back until I began to choke. My version of what it felt like to be a lonely wolf, eating bitter, tiny hermit crabs on a cold, wet, wind-swept beach, bellowed forth and filled the tiny pilothouse. I practiced until my neck almost slipped a disc.

I finally tired of watching the wolf and turned to making up extra leaders, polishing spoons and tying new leaders for bait. Many chores pile up on a troller when one is the cook, deck hand, mate, dishwasher and last, but not least, the captain. The sink seemed perpetually full of dirty dishes, a fathometer needed to be repaired, and other odd jobs awaited me in the engine room. I was tempted to forget the chores and go back to sleep for the duration of the storm, but if I slept all day I'd have trouble sleeping through the long night. I forced myself to do the dreary chores. When finished, I sat by the window to watch the ever-changing scene around my anchored vessel. The wind swirled through the narrow opening to the harbor, sculpturing the restless surface of the water. A bedraggled sea gull, tired of bucking the wind, settled on my bow. He tucked his head under his wings and stood in quiet resignation. Some of the wildest and most beautiful scenery in America spun slowly by the windows as my boat turned on the anchor.

A ragged, V-shaped flock of Canadian geese straggled over the harbor. Their destination was a low pass through the peaks on Baker Island. I watched with profound admiration the maneuverings used by the birds to relieve the strain of bucking the wind. A continuous trading of positions took place, both up and down the two legs of the V and back and forth across it.

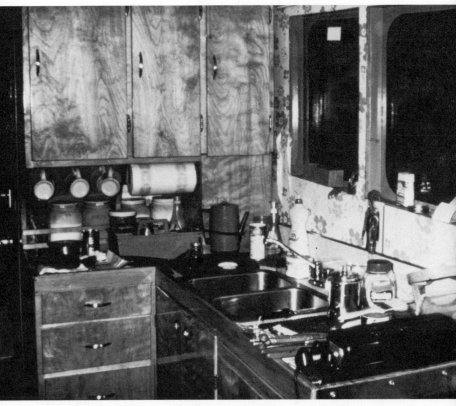

The galley of the Donna C *has all the comforts of home. In the right foreground is a good-sized stove fueled by diesel oil. Large windows afford a good view of the action on deck and beyond.*

I opened the window and listened to their gregarious gossip. Several of the eldest birds were complaining, probably about the too-strenuous pace. Then the flock was out of earshot. I watched them struggle slowly through the pass.

Wild geese, like salmon fishermen, are nomads—always on the move. North in summer, south in winter, these beautiful creatures with the speckled shirts and gun-blue coats have wingspreads of 6 feet. I looked upward longingly, watching the flock with a twinge of jealousy. "If only I had wings like that, the sights I could see, the places I could go. . . ."

Hanging in the fo'c'sle was my Model 70 Winchester. The rifle was chambered for 7mm Remington Magnum and equipped with a 3x9 telescope sight. I brought the rifle up and stood it in the corner by the door. The wolf was still on the beach, howling and coming my way.

After an early supper of spuds, boiled with their jackets on, crab salad and thick steaks off a fat king salmon, I filled my coffee cup and sat by the window. The weather had moderated and the rain had ceased. Then I saw the wolf. He had moved to a point almost straight across the harbor. A half-mile of curved beach lay between us. I timed his howls: one every 4 minutes.

I rubbed the muscles in the back of my neck, stepped on deck and let go with what I hoped sounded like the lament of a very lonesome wolf. I was amazed to see the wolf trot toward me. He covered a hundred yards, then stopped and stared intently in my direction. I let go with another howl, even more lonely than the first.

He placed his broomed tail between his legs and trotted along the beach, evidently delighted that at last he'd called one of his brethren. Again he stopped, sat down and howled.

Behind my anchorage, a small stream gurgled from the spruce forest. The mouth of the creek had deep, gravel banks, about 200 yards away. If the wolf moved up on top of a bank, I would have a reasonable chance for a shot—although the boat wasn't the steadiest platform from which to shoot. Still, I could almost see the tanned hide draped across the back of the sofa in my den at home and hear my friends admire the pelt as they ran their fingers through the soft fur.

Suddenly, near the cutbank on the far side of the creek, I saw movement. I swung the binoculars. There were two black brants. They stood 20 feet apart on the beach, craning their long necks toward the wolf.

"You guys better take off, " I said aloud, "or you'll become that wolf's dinner." Evidently the brants didn't understand English because they merely turned their long necks inquisitively.

Dusk settled slowly over the harbor. The wolf, a handsome

fellow with calico sides, chocolate legs and black ruff and tail, was taking his time. When he was within 20 yards of the brants, they moved. Instead of erupting into the evening sky, they disdainfully stepped aside a few yards and stopped.

Perhaps it was a scheme. The wolf would pretend he was not interested, then when almost past . . .wham . . . blood, guts and feathers. But the wolf just walked between them without a glance, as if they didn't exist.

While I was pondering this quirk of animal nature, a fourth animal appeared. A dark-brown mink was leisurely humping his way down the beach not far from the brants. He stopped within 50 feet of the wolf and began rummaging through some seaweed.

"This is like a Disney movie," I muttered. A wolf, a mink and two black brants, all within the field of my glasses.

The light was fading. The wolf entered the creek mouth and disappeared. I went out on deck and howled again, and took the rifle into the trolling hatch to wait. Darkness cut the visibility. Soon my eyes were streaming from the cold wind and the strain. I waited until I could no longer see the beach, then gave up and went to bed. Several times during the night I awoke and heard him howling. The wind had dropped to a sigh.

At daylight I listened to the Annette Island weather forecast. Another gale was due. Perhaps I could get a few hours' fishing in between gales. When I hauled the anchor, I saw the wolf again. He was at about the same place I'd first spotted him the day before.

Between us a wooded point jutted out into the harbor. If I rowed ashore behind that point I could walk through the timber. When I emerged on the other side I would be within rifle range. It would be almost a cinch to get a shot at him.

It took only a minute to cruise toward the beach behind the point. I let out only enough chain to keep the boat from drifting, then rowed ashore in my light fiberglass skiff. I slid the skiff up on the sand and sprinted toward the timber. Stupid wolf, I thought. He had come to my call and hung around with an anchored boat in plain sight all afternoon and night.

When close to the beach on the other side of the wooded point, I began to crawl on my hands and knees through the tangled windfalls, devil's club and huckleberry bushes. I snagged my pants on a root. I inched along, poking my rifle ahead to be ready for the shot. But the beach was empty.

Thoroughly discouraged, I got to my feet and tromped back through the woods. As I crashed through the last brush and stumbled out onto the beach, a movement near the skiff brought me up short. It was the wolf. He had been investigating my skiff while I'd been stalking him. I threw the rifle to my shoulder.

Suddenly I discovered it wasn't important that I kill the wolf. What mattered was that I could kill him. I had caught him out in the open, fair and square. So I had won, hadn't I?

I stomped to my skiff angrily. Out on the boat, I hauled anchor and proceeded full speed toward Cape Bartolome, some 5 miles away. Probably Vince already had caught several kings while I was fooling with the wolf. I cursed the crafty rascal. He had caused me much embarrassment.

As it turned out, Vince hadn't caught anything, and before the day was over a gale drove us back to San Antonio. We managed to tie our boats together by dropping both anchors. We were still there the next day, talking and fishing for crabs. About noon Vince saw a movement on the beach and reached for the binoculars.

"Wolves," he said. "Two of them."

"Three," I corrected. "One on the sand, another on that gravel bar and the third standing on the large boulders behind."

"Four," Vince announced.

There were more wolves than either of us had ever seen, and we were both excited.

"All that howling last night evidently did some good," I said. "It must have brought him company."

Vince studied the wolves. "There is $200 bounty, just waiting for us."

I hadn't thought about it that way. At the time, the state paid $50 a pelt. And so far we hadn't even made fuel costs from our fishing. We took our rifles and slid the skiff overboard.

"Didn't know wolves were so dumb," I whispered as we rowed ashore. "They just lie there in plain sight."

We worked our way through the dense brush under the timber and edged out to where we could get good open shots. The beach was empty. We walked for a mile or so, looking for glass floats.

We saw only broken glass where several had struck the rocks, and no sign of the wolves.

That night the gale came from the southeast and grew worse during the next 2 days. Our anchors dragged, and to keep from being blown ashore, we set off on a wild ride to Craig, where we could tie up to something solid.

It was just as well. If we somehow had managed to collect that $200, the money would have been long gone. Neither do I think the novelty of a hide draped across the back of a sofa would be quite so valuable as the lifetime memory of those magnificent wolves in the wild.

Forecast: 'Light and Variable'

Weather, the most important element in the salmon and albacore trolling business, can make or break a troller. Tune in on the marine bands. It's the odd conversation that isn't spiced with comments about weather conditions.

Salmon trolling is a delicate business with weather conditions at their best. When the wind blows it can turn into an ordeal that tests the mettle of the most patient person. The light nylon leaders blow off the stern after having been coiled, and the resulting mess must be painstakingly unraveled with fingers numbed by the cold. In addition, the boat becomes nearly unmanageable, wanting to turn and crab every which way when running before the wind, and bouncing up and down like a Yo-Yo while tacking into the seas. If it's blowing hard, many boats find it impossible to run slow enough when going before the wind to let the gear work properly. Spoons and flashers must travel at a certain speed.

Bow poles, especially those pointed far forward, flop up and down with the heavy leads. This often causes fish to be jerked off the hook and the leaders become tangled around the wire. Tempers turn short. Float bags chafe the wire, causing tight curls and kinks that must be cut out and spliced.

Nevertheless, some of the boats stay out fishing even when the seas are running high. It takes a lot of bad weather to drive some fishermen off—if there's good fishing. I've seen men continue to operate during a regular gale. They're the tough guys, the hungry ones.

In a few areas it's possible to troll in the lee of some point of land or cape when the wind blows. This is sometimes done around Noyes Island, if the wind is blowing easterly and thus offshore. Some boats also fish Veta Bay when a gale is blowing. Surface winds are often violent but sea conditions are tolerable. Bob Gay, trolling in the *Suzie M* off The Haystack above Cape Addington one windy day, said on the spook, "It's blowing so hard over here it takes 10 minutes for a flasher to hit the water after you toss it out."

Most fishermen are good forecasters. They look knowingly at the evening and morning skies, cloud formations, the barometer's fluctuations, and watch the actions of sea birds. Birds can sense an approaching storm. Gulls, for instance, almost always fly in circles high in the sky before a strong wind. But the clouds furnish the mariner's best clues.

The fishermen's favorite target when venting their displeasure about foul weather is the weather forecaster. Because he is far away in some warm office, the forecaster is often verbally assaulted. The harassment is good-natured. But it is frustrating to lie for days behind some cape, waiting for storms to go around, listening to a forecast that continues to promise good weather. Sometimes the forecaster is accused of placing a taped forecast on the turntable, while he sneaks away to warmer climates. In Southeastern Alaska it is often said the weatherman has two tapes. One, in use most of the year goes, "Winds fresh southeasterly with higher local gusts and continued rain." The other is used sparingly during late summer just to fool people and make them think he is on the job. It says, "Winds light and variable. Occasional patches of sunshine."

When the forecast is "light and variable" is when fishermen wonder the most about the forecaster's abilities to predict the weather. Long ago the term was translated by some wag to "white and terrible." On more than one occasion this has proved to be true and many who were fishing the Fairweather grounds in 1963 will remember when the forecaster gave us the business with his cheery "light and variable."

My son Dale and I were on the West Bank of the Fairweather Ground, 48 miles from Lituya Bay. The fishing was fair and the kings were good sized. According to the entries in my log, the glass had been dropping steadily for 24 hours.

On the night of May 28, we fished late. At 9 P.M. we listened to Yakutat's KRU-55. The forecast sounded O.K. There were a few lows swishing around the gulf, but it sounded as though we might escape unmolested, which was welcome news. The spring had been a windy one. Of the previous 28 days we had fished only 7. The remainder of the time had been spent behind Cape Fairweather, or in Lituya Bay, or in Pelican, or in between. Several real ripsnorters had lashed the area. After we'd pulled the gear that night, I ran to the East Bank, just in case. The East Bank is only 35 miles from Lituya and a much better position from which to charge madly for the bay in case of a gale. After crossing the gulley between the two banks, I saw the lights of drifting boats and shut down. The night was almost calm. A big lump rolled in from the south, though, and the weather felt threatening. A few of the wise old-timers had gone into Lituya Bay just in case.

The morning of the 29th dawned with a blaze of reddish, streaky clouds. There were fewer boats around because more weather-wise skippers had slid toward the beach during the night. I tapped the barometer. It dropped a tenth of a point.

I had never been in a tough one, but I knew it was going to blow. Needing the money, however, I intended to put out the gear until the 7 A.M. weather report. There wasn't a breath of wind, sometimes a sign that it is going to blow. I put on the coffee and turned on the spook. There was much speculation going on over the air about the weather among the couple of dozen boats still in the area.

I went to the trolling hatch and put out the spoons. By the time all six lines were out, there was a breeze from the southeast. I went inside, just as a salmon jerked a bow line. I called Dale to get up, changed course directly for the bay and went to get the fish. When I stepped on deck, the wind was really whistling. In no time at all this could be nasty, I thought, looking at the great gray lump rolling under us. I stood on deck, trying to figure out what to do. The forecast was due. I went back inside and poured a cup of coffee. The spook was strangely silent; everyone was waiting for the weather. Then, with much static and crackling noise, the announcement came:

"From Dixon Entrance to Sitka, small-craft warnings. From Sitka to Cape Spencer, fresh southeasterlies backing to southerlies by tonight. For Cape Spencer to Yakutat, winds light and variable, becoming south to southeasterly tonight, 10 to 20."

Dale and I looked at each other in disbelief. A nasty sea was already throwing spray over our windward rail against the window. Regardless of the forecast, several boats took off running. The vessels that were still trolling were pointed east.

"Let's get the gear up," I said, struggling into a warm coat and oilskins.

The wind whipped the leaders every which way as we tried to coil them on deck. It was a relief to get inside and speed up. I looked back to where Dale was cleaning the few fish we had caught. Spray was flying off the side of the boat, blowing into his face and down his neck inside his oilskins.

The *Neskowin* called the *Greta* on 2638. The *Neskowin*'s skipper, Roy De Britts, said he hadn't liked the way the barometer was acting. "About 2 A.M. I got up and tapped the glass. It took such a dive I cranked up and headed for town. I didn't want to get trapped in Lituya again. We're almost off the La Perouse Glacier now."

Toivo Anderson replied, "That sounds like a good place to be. Better than this. I think we're all going to be snug and cozy in the bay before long."

By the time we finished breakfast we were off the bank and into deep water. The wind had let up and the seas had stopped, but the lump was still there. I listened to more talk. When the wind slacked, some decided to head for the Inside Bank off Cape Fairweather. There was a chance they could work there the rest of the day and possibly go into the bay that night if the weather warranted it.

"Sounds like a good plan," I told Dale. "Tell you what. I didn't get to bed until 11 P.M., and I'm beat. You take a wheel watch and I'll hit the sack until we reach the edge of the Inside

The author's old boat, the Laverne II *(left), and Harold Chaney's* Valentine *with trolling poles rigged out, fishing before 15,320-foot Mt. Fairweather, which dominates this part of the Alaska coast. If the summit is clear, the fisherman can be assured of several days of good weather. But if he only goes out to the banks when it is clear, he will be likely to fish less than a month out of each year.*

Bank. If the wind comes up again or anything important is said over the radio, call me.'' I fell into my bunk and went to sleep.

Dale's foot-kicking woke me. I got up and climbed to the wheelhouse. The sky was a peculiar bluish black and on the eastern horizon was an ominous wall of grayish storm scud. The wind was gusting to about 40 knots and a sharp sea was causing us to heel far over on our beam ends.

"Where are the other boats?" I asked, looking around. Not a single boat was in sight. What I did see was a white wall of water far to the southeast. It looked like a great breaking wave, and was, in fact, many waves under the rapidly advancing storm front.

"They changed course back there a ways," Dale said. He looked frightened.

"Turned? Why didn't you turn with them?"

He shrugged. "I didn't want to wake you."

As I changed course for the bay, the bow plunged badly in the steep seas. "We're in for trouble."

I spoke into the CB mike. "Pick me up, Roger?" Roger Bailey had been alongside in his *Karolee* when I had hit the sack.

"You bet, Frank," he said. "How are you doing?"

"O.K. so far. Where did you fellows go? I took a nap. When I got up everyone had disappeared."

"Then you didn't hear the *Neskowin*? Roy said a wall of wind and water struck him off the glacier. He's headed back. I'm headed for the bay as fast as this Jimmy will take me."

"What's the tide doing on the bar?"

"It's still flooding. For about an hour. I don't think we're going to make it, Cap."

"The wind just hit a few minutes ago," Dale said.

The storm front struck like a falling brick wall, more wind than I'd ever been caught in before. The first gust laid the boat over on her side and held her there. I changed course toward the southeast. Water whipped over the bow and struck the windows like buckshot. The storm scud thickened until visibility was cut to half a mile. The wind became such a high-pitched scream that talk on the radio was difficult.

"How do you like this, Cap?" I heard someone say over the Mickey.

"I don't. I'd give anything to be in the bay."

Every fifth to seventh sea was fearsome. I had to slow down to keep the windows from breaking. When the boat lifted on a crest and the full sweep of the wind struck us, the bow would swing sideways and I'd have to open the throttle wide to make her answer the rudder. Then another sea would come crashing down.

The tops of the large waves were bent over and the crests blew off. The spindrift found its way through doors, drop windows and down the exhaust system and into the stovepipe. Water sloshed back and forth in the galley.

The *Neskowin* came on the air again. "I'm off Lituya Bay," Roy said. "The bar is breaking clear across. We're sure taking a ride on the rip outside. I'm heading on toward Cape Fairweather.''

This was dismaying news. Lituya was the only harbor available, and it was closed for the next 6 hours, possibly more, depending on the weather. We had no choice now but to turn and head for the slight protection of Cape Fairweather, some 15 miles up the coast.

I waited for a lull to change course. None came. Instead, a wave much greater than any before caught the boat in its grip. It broke clear over the top of the house. The vessel pitched like a bucking bronco and I was thrown to the deck. Water poured off the housetop. I heard a crash in the engine room. By the time I struggled to my feet, we were pointed northeast. I spun the wheel to kick the stern into the next oncoming sea before the vessel broached. Cans of food scattered on the galley deck, along with rolled up charts and broken glassware. A jar of jam spilled. We ignored the mess, walking through it as best we could.

"Check the stove," I said. "See if the fire's out."

Dale shook his head. "It's still going."

I heard Roger shout something to Harold Chaney. "You'd better look out, Harold. A big one just caught me and spun me around. Now I'm pointed toward the cape . . . but that's the way I wanted to go anyway."

There was no answer from the *Valentine*.

Running before the wind we rode easier. "At this rate," I said, "we'll be up to the cape in no time."

Dale nodded. He was standing by the stove, holding onto the sill of the port galley window.

I speeded up. Each wave lifted us high in the air, threatening to break over the after deck. I was thankful the trolling hatch was tightly covered. As we slid down the mountainous seas, the boat would pick up speed. In the troughs I had to steer carefully to keep the boat from spinning around on her bow and broaching.

Suddenly an unusually large wave picked us up. Higher and higher we went. My heart almost stopped when I looked over the bow and saw the awful chasm below. It appeared to be almost straight down, 100 feet deep. "Look out!" I yelled.

The boat plunged headlong into the gigantic trough. When we struck bottom we were going about 15 knots. The bow yawed and

When the seas begin to build and the "white horses" march across the wave tops, the prudent fisherman keeps a sharp eye out for signs and takes the reassuring weather report with a grain of salt.

we broached badly. I'm not sure exactly what happened. I was thrown against the port bulkhead and I remember crouching there on my hands and knees. Then, somehow, the boat righted herself. While she was on her side I heard and felt a sickening thud in the engine room beneath me.

I glanced at Dale as I reached for the throttle and wheel. He was still standing at the window. His face was white.

"Our poles," I shouted. "Did we break a pole?" I looked out. I couldn't see the starboard pole, but the port pole was there.

"The starboard is still there, too," Dale shouted. "It broke the hold-down and has blown up against the mast. I'd better go out and see if I . . ."

"Wait," I cried. I threw the engine out of gear and put on my oilskins. When I opened the door slightly a torrent of wind came through the crack. "I'm going out to pull the haul-up lines. Keep an eye on me."

The wind on deck was like a knife. Before I'd untangled the lines and tightened them, my eyes were dimmed by spray and wind. A quick look up the mast confirmed my fears. The pole had missed its bracket as it resettled and was leaning against the mast. As I struggled to tighten it, I looked across at the other pole. It was flopping badly with its stays hanging loose.

I slid the door open. "I'm going to have to pull the other pole. I'll probably break it when it comes against the mast, but it's stretched the stays or something and is going to cause all sorts of trouble the way it is."

Dale nodded. "When we laid over it disappeared underwater."

I waited for a chance to hoist the 42-foot pole without breaking it. The ugly swells lifted their towering gray heads over us, each threatening to crash down and smash our small craft to bits. The boat lifted, however, and with a sickening lurch crossed the top of each sea, only to slide sideways down the other side.

"Put her in forward. Try to hold her stern into the seas. And don't speed up too much."

On deck I held the haul-up lines. When we were at the bottom of a trough I let the pole out, released the hold-down and pulled as fast as I could. The pole slammed upward. Suprisingly it lodged in the pole bracket on the mast without breaking.

Inside the galley I wiped sea water from my face. "Lucky! Saved both poles," I grinned. "Now I'll go see what happened in the engine room."

The auxiliary generating plant had been torn loose from its mount on one side of the engine room and now lay upside down on the opposite side. I lashed it where it lay. I noticed the exhaust pipe was coated white—salt from sea water that had blown down the stack.

"Light plant tore loose," I shouted to Dale. "Everythings's O.K. now." I engaged the clutch and started out again. We hadn't gone far when we came upon a vessel drifting in a trough. One pole was missing and the other was upright.

"Looks like the *Valentine*," I said. I reached for the mike. "Pick me up, Harold? Everything O.K.?"

When there was no answer I steered toward the vessel. Harold was struggling on the main deck attempting to retrieve the broken pole and its rigging. He looked up at us and waved.

"*Laverne II. Karolee* calling. What's the matter? Is Harold in trouble?"

"Broken pole, Roger. He's on deck, trying to get the junk aboard."

"O.K. I wondered when I didn't hear him answer back."

"I think his antenna was knocked down when the pole broke. I don't see it," I said.

"All right. Let me know if you find out anything."

"He's trying to pull the pole aboard and lash it," Dale said.

"I hope none of the rigging gets in the wheel." I steered slowly toward the *Valentine*.

Harold disappeared inside the pilothouse and the *Valentine* slowly started for the cape.

"Look," Dale said. "There's a bunch of trolling gear, leaders, wire and stuff hanging over the stern."

I reached for the mike. "Harold, there's a big bunch of flashers and trolling wire hanging over your stern. I know your antenna is down but you can probably hear this over the antenna lead-in wire."

"What's going on over there?" Roger asked.

"Everything is O.K. We're proceeding toward the cape. The *Valentine* is right ahead of us. He's got the pole lashed on deck."

Within an hour we could see the low, dark outline of the cape. When we reached the anchorage several boats were already there. Some had poles missing. The surface winds were very strong, probably 60 knots. I let the anchor go. Forty fathoms of chain went flying out and the boat fetched up with a snap. A large swell rolled under us. We were rolling so badly it was difficult to stand up. I watched the shore for a few minutes to make sure we weren't dragging anchor.

"I'm going to hit the sack for a while," I said. "It may be a long night if it keeps this up."

"Me too," Dale said.

The wind in the rigging and the jerking and snapping of the anchor chain prevented me from sleeping, tired as I was. I lay in a daze, worrying that the wind might switch to southwest, turning the anchorage into a deathtrap.

Every hour or so I got up. More boats were joining us. The *Trader II,* belonging to Harold Johnson, came in missing a pole. I turned on the radio and listened to a conversation between the

The Aloha *lies behind the scant protection of Cape Fairweather, Alaska. Wide open to the swells that sweep in, this is a rolly, uncomfortable anchorage, good only in calm weather or as a last resort when you can't get in anywhere else.*

Deep Sea and the *Lightly.* The *Deep Sea* was in trouble. She had been running in to shelter when a deck hose washed into the open trolling hatch. The aft section had filled up and skipper Art Theberge was trying to bail it out with a bucket.

John Clauson on the *Lightly,* a 58-footer built under John's careful instructions and with two 6-71 GMC diesels, sat snug and cozy in Lituya Bay. Art's predicament worried John. He pulled his anchor and cruised over to the *Pat,* a troller anchored nearby. "Dick," he yelled to the skipper, "I think I'll go out and stand by Art. He could be in serious trouble with that much water in the stern. But I need a hand. I wouldn't be much help alone."

Bob Smith, who was working on the *Pat,* grabbed his oilskins and jumped on board the *Lightly.*

"The bar is breaking," Dick said. "How are you going to cross it?"

"Oh," John yelled, "we'll just have to find a hole." Then he headed for the bar. He stayed out of the center of the channel and kept close along the inside of La Chaussee Spit. The tide was ebbing over the shallow bar at a rapid rate. When it met the swells coming in from outside, it reacted violently by rising up in huge seas, then breaking heavily. John watched the oncoming swells. After a while he thought he saw a pattern. Timing it carefully, he speeded up and reached the center of the bar just as a smaller-than-usual swell was approaching.

"Hang on!" John yelled.

Bob was already hanging on. Ahead was a wild, white hell.

Water broke over the *Lightly* from bow to stern covering the windows. It was impossible to see. The vessel rose high in the air and nose-dived.

"We made it," John yelled. Now all that remained was to run in the trough some 15 miles out to where the *Deep Sea* was drifting.

Another vessel, Ralph Mortenson's little *Totem,* was still out in the gale a few miles downwind of the *Deep Sea.* Without a moment's hesitation Ralph turned from his course to the cape and also began inching into the murderous wind toward the *Deep Sea.*

I went back to bed. When I got up, I heard that the *Deep Sea* was on her way into the bay under her own power. The *Blithe Spirit,* however, was in a bad spot on the West Bank. Her skipper, Lloyd Gowdy, had tried running with his stabilizers out when the wind had first struck. Both poles came down, and stay wires and rigging surrounded the boat. Seas were churning across the deck. It wasn't safe outside, Lloyd decided, so he did the wisest thing possible—he went to bed, figuring that the wind was going to die down sometime. It was so rough he couldn't have made much headway even if he had managed to get all the debris aboard.

John Clauson's Lightly *trolling on a typical gray day off Khaz Bay, Alaska, about 45 miles south of Cape Spencer.*

At daylight the boats started pulling their anchors. Down at Lituya the tide would be flooding into the bay, causing the bar to level off enough to enter.

My anchor was buried so deep I had difficulty breaking it out. After 45 minutes of running up on top of the buried anchor, having the big swell fetch the boat up solid on the short length of chain and still failing to break it out, I was about ready to cut it loose. The bulwarks, where the anchor roller was mounted on the bow, were starting to pull away from the stem with the strain. In the engine room I found a turnbuckle and jury-rigged it on the anchor roller. The next time I took in chain the anchor broke out, but it was twisted beyond use. Luckily I had a spare.

Bucking to the bay wasn't very pleasant. The wind had died some, but a wicked sea was still running. We kept close to the shore in 10 fathoms. This route is known locally as the "mink trail" and is much used, both between the cape and the bay, and the bay and Icy Point during bad weather.

At 7 A.M. we were abreast of the entrance bar. The flood swept us quickly through. About 30 boats were anchored there, many of them missing poles, hatch covers and skiffs. We spent that day and the next resting, eating, tightening and repairing stays on the poles and cleaning up the mess—generally known as "licking our wounds."

The following morning we crossed the bar hoping to fish. The wind was still blowing lightly from the southeast and a leftover lump made sea conditions miserable. The forecast was for more southeasterlies that night. Reluctantly we turned and headed for Pelican and were storm bound there for the next 4 days. Several of the boats had made their way 50 miles out to the West Bank only to get hit with another gale almost as bad as the one we had been caught in. More poles were broken, windows smashed, and the fleet was forced back into the bay.

Dale and I nervously paced up and down Pelican's main street, half a mile of boardwalk. We were thankful to be there but also anxious to get back out fishing. We soothed ourselves with many trips to the steam bath.

On June 6 we left Cape Spencer and ran offshore toward the East Bank all day. "It's June now," I told Dale. "The weather just has to settle down. Maybe we'll get a good trip this time."

We arrived on the grounds in time to go to bed. By late afternoon the next day we were once more charging for the shelter of Lituya Bay. Another southeaster was blowing, and as we neared the coast the tide was ebbing again. This time, though, it wasn't blowing so hard, and by running slowly, we wouldn't have to wait too long at the bar for slack water.

Late that night we entered the bay and dropped anchor behind The Paps. I stood on the fo'c'sle deck in the cold, driving rain and studied the angle of the anchor chain. A 30-knot wind was blowing from the head of the bay and a sea was running. Sometimes I was fairly sure the mast lights on the other anchored boats were moving. This meant my spare anchor was dragging. I cursed silently. What I needed most was sleep, but you can't sleep knowing the anchor is dragging.

I picked up the anchor, ran ahead and reset it. This time I let out all the chain. Cold rain whipped at my face as I waited to see if it was going to hold. I stood with one hand on the forestay and a booted foot on the chain—feeling it with my foot. If there were vibrations, it was dragging. If it remained steady it probably wasn't. I tried to visualize the anchor on the bottom. Was it buried in soft mud? Clay? Perhaps it was lying on a smooth stretch of solid rock? Possibly it was hung up behind a large boulder. It might slip off the rock at any moment, letting us drag.

Chilled to the bone, weary almost beyond caring and thoroughly discouraged by the fishing business, I went into the galley and removed my oilskins. It had been 22 hours since I'd had any sleep. I sat down by the range. Its welcome heat was a wonderful thing. I thought of Lapp Sam and his wood stove. I made hot chocolate and some toast. Dale was sleeping. I opened the logbook and took stock of the situation. In the past 8 days I'd caught only 18 salmon. I'd traveled almost 400 miles, most of it on an ocean that was almost standing on end. I wrote the daily entry:

"June 7: Fished most of the day on East Bank. 12 kings. S.E. wind came up. Ran into the bay. Tide ebbing. Jogged outside for an hour. Anchored in southeast anchorage at 11 P.M."

For what reason would a man lead such a miserable life? Riches? Certainly not. Glory? What glory? Love? How could anyone love a bitch such as the sea? Why then? I pondered the question, drained my cup, checked the lights on the nearby boats to see if we were dragging anchor and took off my heavy woolen clothes.

Finally, I left the warmth of the galley and crawled into my cramped bunk in the fo'c'sle. The steady drumming of the wind in the rigging assured me there would be no fishing tomorrow and no reason to get up. I pulled the blankets over my head to stifle the sounds of my old enemy the wind, and prepared for a long, long sleep.

Man Overboard

Storms are perils that fishermen take for granted, but it is an irony of their lives that tragedy also can strike when weather and sea are at their best.

The faint glimmer of daybreak seeping through the fo'c'sle skylight wakened me. I lay quietly, feeling the roll of the boat for an indication of the morning weather: the sea felt almost flat. For the tuna grounds, 100 miles off Newport, Oregon, it had been a wonderful night for drifting. The miserable northwest wind that had plagued us for several days had died with the sun. It was August 9, 1966.

Sleepily I climbed the ladder and peered out. The sea's surface was glassy, an oily gray in the faint light. Two white mast lights bobbed and swung gently in the distance. Good, I thought, my two running mates were close by. I pushed the starter button and a rumble came from the diesel below. Its noise, along with a few slaps on each cheek, helped awaken me. I filled the coffeepot, turned on both radios, CB and a 100-watt Raytheon. Last, I turned on my most faithful piece of equipment, a model 11 Freeman automatic pilot.

Having gone through my daily ritual of switch flipping, I went on deck to pump the bilge. Much to my surprise a tiny yellow and brown shore bird—about the size of a golf ball—stood on spindly legs at the end of the pump handle. I reached toward him. He eyed me belligerently and fluffed his wings. "Look here," I said grumpily, "I know you're lost at sea and all that, but I've given you a roost for the night. What more do you want?"

I hated to oust him, but I could hear the bilge alarm ting every time the boat rolled. To my relief the bird decided the top of the double-drum seine winch was a steadier place to perch. I grabbed the pump handle and set to work.

Over my shoulder I noticed the 100 albacore left on deck from the evening before. I groaned inwardly. There'd be work aplenty this morning. Those fish had to be lowered into the hold and iced.

Albacore tuna, called bigeye and longfin by some fishermen, had bitten our feathered jigs savagely just at dusk. As I pumped, the muscles in my sore hands responded painfully. I hoped the fish were still lurking nearby and that we'd have a good morning bite. While I emptied the bilge I contemplated our chances of filling the hold before we were forced in to port and the fish buyer by ice and fuel shortages.

Our hopes had been shaken a few days before when our loran had failed, after being soaked by a sea that had splashed through a window carelessly left open. I knew that without this important instrument it would be difficult for me to home in on hot spots reported on the radio.

Luckily, I had come across two friends, the *Cygnet II* and the *Valentine*. These two vessels and I had already suffered through a skimpy salmon season up in the Cape Fairweather country. We had tired of dodging southeast gales and elusive king salmon and separately had migrated some 800 miles down to the more temperate weather off the Oregon coast. Both boats had loran so I had attached myself to them until I could head for market.

About the time the pump indicated that the bilge was dry, the *Cygnet II* approached. A boil of white water peeled off either side of her bow. Within hailing distance she hove to by backing down abruptly. Erick Lindeman, a long-time Alaskan fisherman, appeared on the bow.

"Good morning, Captain. How do you like this peach-blossom weather? Do you think the fish are still here? Water temperature is 62°."

The well-kept Finn-built boat, Cygnet II, *which belonged to Erick Lindeman, unloading fish at Newport, Oregon.*

I smiled at his exuberance. Erick was a Finn, loved to fish, owned a fine Finn-built boat and had a wonderful family at his home in Ketchikan. In addition, he'd told me a few days before that recently he had made the last payment on his boat, had her in perfect shape and was really enjoying tuna fishing after an almost 20-year absence from the tuna grounds.

"Good," I replied. "With flat and glassy seas we can bail 'em aboard like crazy, if we can find 'em. For that I'm depending on you two hot shots."

"That's why I wanted to see you," Erick shouted. "You've got the large-scale loran chart for this area. All I have is the one that shows the whole coast. I have a heck of a time laying out courses on it. Can I have your chart?"

"Sure, Erick, I'll get it for you. It's no good to me. I can get another one when I get to town." I went in and took the chart off the table, rolled it up and tied it. Hanging in the stays I had a flagpole. (This device is a cane or bamboo pole 18 feet long with a weight on the bottom, a cork float about halfway up, and a red flag on top.) Flagpoles are made for marking the end of a set of halibut longline gear, but at sea we trollers are forever using them for transferring objects, such as mail and spare parts, from one boat to another.

I lashed the chart to the top of the pole and slid it over the side. Then I engaged the clutch and pulled the boat away from the flagpole so that the *Cygnet II* had room to pick it up without our poles tangling. Erick picked up the flagpole and removed the chart. He then tossed the pole back into the sea for me to recover, waved and disappeared into the pilothouse. A cloud of smoke shot skyward as he opened the throttle on the Cummings engine. He was anxious to get his gear into the water for the morning bite.

Also on board the *Cygnett II* was Erick's 16-year-old son Billy. Over on the *Valentine* were veteran troller Harold Chaney, his wife Evelyn and their son Mike, also about 16. My wife Donna and my 14-year-old stepson Vaughn Wilson were with me on our *Laverne II*.

By the time I retrieved the flag the sun was a half-round orange and red ball peeking over the eastern horizon. On my way to the cockpit I noticed the shore bird still sitting dejectedly on the hatch. Ordinarily I would have provided food and water for him but I was in such a hurry to start fishing that I ignored his plight.

From the trolling hatch I hurled five feathered jigs overboard, then moved to the opposite side and put out five more. When I turned around, two of the first five jigs had fish on them.

"Hot dog," I yelled, and began to pull. Before I had pulled them in, there were fish hanging on several more lines. "Whoopee!" I shouted, hoping to wake Donna and Vaughn so they would come help. They didn't. I steered in a large circle. Off to the southeast I could see Erick in the cockpit pulling like mad. The *Cygnet II* was also in a circle.

This'll never do, I thought, doing my best to keep the lines clear. Often fish bite like this for a few minutes at daylight, then sometimes again at night. In between, fishing can be slow. It's a case of get all you can while they're biting. I hurried toward the fo'c'sle. The bird stared at me through half-closed lids as I passed. "Don't die on me, little bird. I'll get around to caring for you. I haven't had my coffee yet, either."

In the fo'c'sle I shook Vaughn. "Gotta have help," I yelled above the engine's rumble. "Fish! All over the place!"

By the time Vaughn joined me the deck was covered with shimmering, quivering bluish silver albacore, their long, scythe-shaped fins wavering. We each took a side and pulled.

Breakfast was a series of gulps topped off with long overdue coffee. Between gulps I peered out the galley window to see what was going on in the cockpit. We were still in a circle. I found it hard to concentrate on the mush because Vaughn yelled like crazy every time he saw another fish hit the lines.

"We're in a mess," I told Donna. She was standing by the galley range holding the bird in one hand and stroking its head with the other. "There are almost two tons of fish on deck, and they have to be iced." I took a full cup of coffee and headed for the trolling hatch.

"O.K.," I told Vaughn. "It's your turn for breakfast." The decks were red with blood and bits of squid and tiny fish disgorged by the tuna. I flung several buckets of water on the deck. The sea behind us turned red. We were still circling.

As the sun climbed higher the bite slowly stopped. Shortly after Vaughn came back out, I saw the *Cygnet II* stop circling and move toward the northwest. I left the trolling hatch and went into the galley. "Donna, you steer. Just follow Erick or Harold. I've got to get down there and ice those fish." She nodded and took the wheel.

I went into the hold. Twenty-five albacore lay waiting. I placed the fish in layers with crushed ice between and over them. Then I crawled out and lowered 25 more. By the time I'd iced the 50 fish I was out of space and had to dig out a bin of ice. It was hard work. I was in the hold over an hour and came out hot, tired and with a backache. I pulled off my oilskin pants and sat down in the galley.

"You look all in," Donna said. "I'll pour you a cup of coffee."

"Thanks. I need something. I got that ton iced. Now there's another hundred or so out there staring me in the face." I sipped the coffee. "What's going on?" I jerked my thumb toward the CB radio.

"Haven't heard a word."

"I guess you know what that means," I said. "Everyone's pulling fish."

Ahead and off to port I could see the *Cygnet II*. There was someone in her trolling hatch. The *Valentine* was way off to the west. I loafed a while. The next time I looked at the *Cygnet II* her hatch was empty.

"I think I'll call Erick and see how he's doing," I said. Before I could reach the mike an excited voice came over the air. It jabbered something that was completely incoherent.

"Who on earth was that?" Donna asked.

"I think it was Billy Linderman." I picked up the mike. "Billy? Was that you? If so, come back slower. We can't read you."

There was a long pause, then, "Frank! Frank! I can't find my dad anywhere on the boat!"

I looked at Donna. Her eyes were wide. There was no doubting the panic in Billy's voice.

"You can't find Erick? He must be there someplace. He couldn't just disappear. Have you looked on the bridge? How about in the head or the engine room?"

"Frank, I've already looked in all those places," he cried.

Donna's hand went to her mouth. Her face was ashen. I remembered times when I had thought my boat puller was missing, only to find him curled up in some unusual place. But there are only so many places on a small boat where a man can hide. Undoubtedly Billy already had searched everywhere.

"Frank. Frank! Are you hearing me all right?" Billy called.

"Yes. Stand by a moment. I have to think." I had to sound calm.

"What am I going to do?"

"Perhaps you'd better start at the beginning," I said.

"All right, I was down in the hold icing fish. I must have been there 45 minutes or an hour. When I came back on deck the lines were all loaded with fish. I yelled for Dad but he didn't answer. I thought he was on the radio talking to you, so I pulled all the fish. There were about a hundred on deck so I threw them down on the ice. I came in here expecting to find him. Then I looked for him. I looked everywhere. I tell you, Frank, he's not aboard the boat. What are we going to do?"

My heart sank. Sometime while Billy had been in the hold Erick had disappeared.

"Billy, don't panic. It's a nice day. If he fell overboard we'll soon find him. Now tell me—when you came into the pilothouse was the automatic pilot in gear?"

"It was running but it wasn't engaged."

"In other words, the *Cygnet II* was finding her own way?"

"Yes. And I have no idea where we've been. Do you?"

"Stand by. I've been in the hold, too. I'll have to talk to Donna."

I turned to my wife. "Donna, I know you're not experienced enough to retrace our course exactly, but I want you to remember as much as you can. Tell me everything that happened. Did we circle? Did the *Cygnet II* circle? Everything, Donna. It's our only hope of backtracking."

"I did what you told me to do. I followed the *Cygnet II* while you were in the hold."

"That's fine. But did anything unusual happen? Did you see Erick out on deck or in the cockpit? Think hard."

"Something funny did happen. If I hadn't been watching we'd have been run down. I looked out the side window and the *Cygnet II* was right there, pointed right toward our middle. I had a devil of a time turning quickly enough."

"Was anyone in the cockpit when she went by?"

"No."

"He was gone then. Erick would never crowd like that. I've fished around him a long time." I picked up the mike. "Billy, let's reverse course. Harold, are you listening?"

"Roger, I've been listening. I was quite a ways off so I couldn't actually add anything. But I took a loran bearing as soon as Billy gave the alarm."

"Good for you, Cap. You're the only one who can keep us on the spot with that loran set. By my calculations we have to search toward the southeast. We'll find him," I added. But I lacked confidence. I knew that Erick, like many other commercial fishermen, had been so busy on top of the ocean making a living that he had never learned to swim. However, many a man who had thought he couldn't swim managed it when about to drown.

Off to starboard the *Cygnet II* went into a hard turn. Smoke shot out of her exhaust. The sea was calm, almost flat. Only a slight swell from the northwest rolled under our boat. How, I wondered, could anyone fall overboard on a day like this?

"Vaughn, climb as high as you can on the mast. Donna, you stand on top of the house. If you see anything, anything at all, sing out!"

I noticed Billy was up on his bridge. He wouldn't be able to hear the radio from there. I called Harold.

"Harold, we're working against tremendous odds because we've wandered all over the place. Billy's up on the bridge and can't hear us. What do you think about putting the news out on 2638? We need boats to cover the whole area. We could have gone 5 or 6 miles since he fell. That's a hell of a lot of ocean to spot a man in."

"Good idea. Maybe you should alert the Coast Guard, too."

I twisted the selector switch on my transmitter to the distress frequency, 2182. High on Cape Disappointment, overlooking the Columbia River bar, perched a Coast Guard lighthouse. The men there were no strangers to emergencies requiring swift action. I pressed the mike button.

"Cape Disappointment Light—Cape Disappointment Light. Troller *Laverne II,* WC 5209, calling Cape Disappointment Light."

"This is Cape Disappointment Light. Vessel calling come in again with your call sign."

"This is the *Laverne II,* WC 5209. I'm reporting a man overboard and requesting assistance—an aircraft to search for him. My position: 170 miles southwest of the Columbia River lightship. My loran lines are 2468 on 1H-4 and 3172 on 1H-5. Sea condition is calm, visibility unlimited."

"Roger your emergency traffic. What is your vessel's length, color of hull and how many persons on board?"

The Coast Guard asked additional questions. To assess the situation in such an emergency, they must ask many seemingly needless questions. It took about 15 minutes for them to get all the information they needed. I was instructed to stand by.

I quickly switched to 2638, the fishermen's band. Hundreds of albacore boats were tuned to this frequency, and the channel was buzzing with the usual comments.

I called for silence for an emergency announcement. After several tries everyone finally got the message.

"We're out here in the middle of the 2,400 block, about 3,170 on 5. Erick Lindeman, skipper of the *Cygnet II,* is missing and presumed to be overboard. We'd like to have help here to look for him. His boat puller was in the hold for about an hour so he's apt to be anywhere within 6 miles of this location."

Right away my friend Don Davis on the *Urania* answered. He repeated my message on his powerful radio so that everyone had a second chance to hear it. He ended with: "O.K., we'll head up that way. We're about 50 miles southeast of you."

Harold was on the CB, to say the Coast Guard was calling me on 2182.

I answered their call. To our relief the highly developed machinery of the Search and Rescue was in motion. An amphibian plane from our hometown of Port Angeles, Washington, the closest Coast Guard Air Detachment, was on its way. I was instructed to stand by for the pilot, to answer his call when he approached and to indicate the center of the search area.

I went on deck. "Any luck?" I asked Donna. She was standing on top of the house, her hand shielding her eyes from the sun.

"Nothing."

"There's a plane coming from P.A. Watch for it."

Vaughn was perched high in the rigging. He hadn't seen anything either.

Several masts appeared on the horizon in response to my message. By the time the plane arrived, more boats had joined the search. The pilot and I made contact. He asked me to place my boat in a tight circle so he could single me out for future reference. Then he asked me to indicate when I was at the center of the area. Soon a smoke flare struck the water. Then the aircraft began a slow series of tight turns. Now, I thought, the next few minutes will tell the tale.

Billy's slender figure could be seen on the bridge of the *Cygnet II*. I knew he was not experienced enough to take loran readings with any degree of accuracy, and I worried about his welfare. A stiff northwest breeze had sprung up and the sky was clear—a sure sign of northwest wind on the tuna grounds. Somehow Billy had to have help. I called the Coast Guard again.

The Atlas, *out of Seattle, Washington, trolling off Cape Fairweather. On most fishing boats a man at the stern is always vulnerable to a slip or to a rogue sea.*

"Billy is experienced around boats," I told them, "but he's not qualified to run the *Cygnet II.* He's an Alaskan, and not acquainted with the dangerous bars along this coast. What's more, it's starting to blow. It's important that someone be placed aboard to assist him right away, before the sea becomes too rough for a boarding. Also, his mother in Ketchikan must be notified."

The Coast Guard agreed to try to assist Billy, but they were reluctant to notify Mrs. Lindeman. They insisted either Billy or I attempt to make the call.

We had been searching for 7 hours. I'm sure none of us had any hope of finding Erick. A wicked sea was now running on a heavy northwest swell. Whitecaps danced across the crest of the waves, making the search impossible. The plane departed as darkness fell. Again and again I tried to call Billy. Finally, at full darkness, I made contact.

"The only good news I have, Billy, is that the Coast Guard is sending the deepsea tug *Modoc*. She's due about daylight."

"That's good. What happens then?"

"It depends on the weather. If possible, they'll put someone aboard to assist you. Then they'll probably escort you into Newport. Now, can you call the Seattle marine operator and place a call to your mother?"

"O.K., I'll try. Give me a few minutes to collect my thoughts—then I'll call her."

Vaughn, Donna and I looked at each other. All our thoughts were with Billy, having to decide how to break the news to his mother. I couldn't help because I didn't have the Seattle frequency on my radio.

We were drifting now. A 15-foot swell tossed us every which way. I went on deck to look around. The night was as black as the inside of a cow. The howl of the wind and the jerking motion of the boat spelled a very uncomfortable night. It was blowing about 30, and if it kept up they could forget about placing a man on the *Cygnet II* in the morning. With my loran out and Billy unable to read his, it would be very easy for us to become separated. Then what?

A while later Billy came in on the radio.

"Frank, I got through to Mom. She's going to fly to Portland tomorrow."

"That's fine, Billy. You've done well. I'll keep your mast light in sight tonight. By daylight perhaps you'll have some help from the *Modoc*."

"I hope so. I'm so tired I can hardly stand up. But I don't think I can sleep."

"I don't wonder," I said. "But try to get some rest. The plane is coming back at daylight. We'll have to be ready to begin the search again tomorrow. Don't worry, I'll keep an eye on you."

Our evening meal was very brief and we ate mechanically. The *Modoc* called. They were encountering heavy weather and requested that I check back at midnight.

At midnight I called the *Modoc*. They had been slowed because of the high seas. The skipper advised me that their E.T.A. was

Dale Caldwell on the after deck of Laverne II *wrestles aboard a nice king salmon on the Goose Island Bank, Queen Charlotte Sound, British Columbia. Fishing is heavy work when you are pulling in the big ones.*

now 9 A.M. The *Cygnet II*'s weaving mast light appeared and disappeared half a mile away. I went to bed and eventually dozed. A sudden bump awakened me. At the after door I saw the cause of the jar—another boat, stern to and about to smash into us again. Automatically I pressed the starter button, engaged the clutch and opened the throttle wide. As the boat moved, I heard a cable snap on deck. Donna sprang out of bed.

"What's the matter?" she exclaimed.

"Collision," I said. "Another boat. A double-ender, didn't get the name. Only saw 'Astoria' on the stern."

I took a flashlight and went aft to survey the damage. A broken pole stay flopped dangerously in the wind and one tag line blew sideways, trailing in the sea. The ironbark guard near the stern was smashed. I leaned over and shined the light across the hull planking, very conscious that only an inch and a half of Alaska cedar lay between us and the cruel green sea. Somehow, on a night like this, that thin wood seemed inadequate. Seeing no additional damage, I peered back at the other boat. Its pilothouse was dark. Evidently its captain hadn't even been awakened by the jar. I checked the hold. There was only the normal amount of water in the bilge. With a sigh of relief I rejoined Donna in the pilothouse.

"We're lucky. Only minor damage."

I engaged the clutch and jogged into the wind to place some distance between us. When we were about a mile away I shut down the engine and walked on deck to look around. As far as I could see in the starlight, a procession of marching, white-capped giants bore down on us. Why, I wondered, would anyone do this sort of work for a living?

Dawn arrived with a brassy glow in the east. The sea was not pretty. I dreaded to think how far we had drifted during the night.

"Good morning, Billy," I said into the CB mike. I had told him to leave the set on all night.

"Yes, yes, I get you fine," Billy said sleepily.

"Did you get any rest?"

"Not much—but I feel better than I did last night. What are we going to do?"

"Well, first of all, the *Modoc* had to slow down. She's due at about 9 o'clock. We're going to try and locate each other. Another boat banged into us last night and I got separated from you. Do you see me this morning?"

A long pause, then, "No. I don't see you or the *Valentine.* "

"I have a schooner about 2 miles south. Do you see her?"

"No. All I see is a black steel boat. It's upwind from me."

"O.K. That black boat is about 2 miles east of me. You come west-northwest. You'll soon be able to see me. Now, if Harold's listening, maybe he'll tell us how far we drifted last night."

"Good morning, Frank and Billy," Harold said. "We drifted 8 miles south. I'm already jogging back up. I'll take it easy until you two catch up."

I turned up the radio. A short period of listening disclosed that many in the fleet had worked toward shelter because they thought it was really going to blow. But the fickle northwester fooled us all. By the time the *Modoc* arrived, the wind had dropped to a breeze. The plane from Port Angeles was back and, having spotted a floating object, dropped a smoke flare. The pilot asked for the nearest boat to check it out.

For an instant, hope was rekindled. Then the boat reported that the object was driftwood. I called the *Modoc* and insisted they put someone on board to help Billy as soon as possible. At noon an officer boarded the *Cygnet II*. We all were greatly relieved. Soon the *Cygnet II* was heading for Newport. The search was officially called off and everyone was released to continue whatever they had been doing.

We found the *Valentine* and tossed out the feathered jigs again, but there were no fish. For us, as for other fishermen, the search hadn't ended—only the object had changed. About 30 miles to the west, we heard, boats were scoring 50 albacore. We pointed our bows in that direction.

A few days later we tied up to Hugo and Elna Seeborg's oil dock in Astoria. Wearily I climbed the steel rungs of the ladder, entered Hugo's office and sagged into his familiar old horsehair sofa.

Hugo looked at me. "Rough trip?"

"You heard what happened."

Hugo shook his head sadly. He went into the back room and returned with a bottle of whiskey. He poured us both a drink. "Too bad about Lindeman."

"Here's to a fine man," I said, raising my glass. "But what a hell of a way to go. He'd just paid off the mortgage on that boat and had it in top shape."

Hugo cleared his throat. "The Finns have a saying, 'A boatless man is a man in chains.'"

"What does that have to do with it?" I asked.

"You said it was a hell of a way to go. But stop and think a moment. Lindeman loved fishing and boats. He died happy, doing what he loved to do."

"I'll drink to that, Hugo."

And we did.

Jess Remodels His Boat

Big Jess Payton, who lived in Port Alexander, owned the schooner *Repeat*. Jess is a raw-boned man with cauliflower ears which, with his frame and clublike fists, indicated he didn't get those ears from being mauled by a bear. Jess Payton is an ex-boxer. He is amenable enough despite his fierce appearance. At the time, had a great black beard that hung down to his massive chest.

Jess fished off Baranof Island and came to Sitka to unload. After a few beers with Beamy Fredrickson and other friends at the Pioneer Bar, he would outfit for a trip and head home for a couple of days before striking out again to his favorite fishing grounds off Whale Bay or Necker Bay.

Sitka, the old capital of Russian America, is blessed with a beautiful setting. The town lies on a flat bench, with Harbor Peak, the saw-toothed peaks of The Sisters and pyramid-shaped Verstovia and Arrowhead as a backdrop. Seaward from the town are scattered stepping-stone-sized islands. To the west is the dormant volcano, Mt. Edgecumbe, an Alaskan Fujiyama which, on a bright day, is alone worth a trip to Sitka. Beyond the peak are the famous trolling grounds off Cape Edgecumbe.

Besides being an unloading center for salmon and halibut, Sitka is the main supply center for an area from Cape Decision to Cape Spencer. Pelican has a cold-storage plant and is 60 miles closer to the Fairweather grounds, but it lacks medical facilities and some necessary supplies.

Late one afternoon when not many boats were in, the *Repeat* unloaded at Sitka Cold Storage. Big Jess took his fishing money and went uptown to "splice the main brace." Before leaving he gave his deck hand orders to wash down the hold and move the boat across to the float. The deck hand moved the schooner and tied her at the float, stern to and hard by The Galley restaurant. Then he wandered off to see the bright lights himself.

Among those of us in The Galley this particular evening were Marlus Korlach, who owned the *Condor* and later was manager of La Push Fish Company in La Push, Washington; Keen Gou of the *Bluejacket*; Howard "Red" Rawley, then the jovial owner of the *Democrat*; Glen Smith of the schooner *Stamsund* (Glen and Red traded boats later); and Beamy Fredrickson, long-time Alaskan and proud owner of the smart little double-ender *JoAnn*. The Galley, since torn down, was a ramshackle little restaurant that perched high on rickety pilings and overlooked the cold-storage float. Because it was handy and served excellent seafood and homemade pies, many of us fishermen ate there.

About the time we finished eating, Big Jess ambled in, red-eyed and a bit unsteady. He sat down and ordered black coffee.

Beamy pointed down to where the *Repeat* was tied, and asked, "Why don't you build a new pilothouse, Jess? Here you've got a 50-foot boat, and the house is so small you have to back outside to get your hands in your pockets."

Big Jess nodded. "Been thinking about it. Like to make the new one large enough so I can move the oil range up from the fo'c'sle. We could cook up there. Be handier."

"I don't know about that," Glen Smith said, chewing his cigar. "In cold weather that old fo'c'sle can be pretty warm and comfy with a good stove in it."

"That's for sure," Jess agreed. "Well, the thing to do is leave the stove in the fo'c'sle and buy a new one for the house on deck."

Traveler II, Aloha *and* Laug *at the wharf, Sitka Cold Storage. Old automobile tires make good fenders to protect the hull from damage when mooring alongside another boat or to a dock.*

Everyone nodded. It was settled. Sometime, whenever Jess could catch enough fish to afford it, the *Repeat* would have a splendid new house with a galley. Talk returned to the usual—lousy weather, poor prices and the scarcity of fish. Soon Big Jess rose to leave. "Time to check the boat," he said.

We watched Jess wobble down the ramp and crawl on board. Instead of heading for his bunk in the fo'c'sle, he stepped inside the wheelhouse door and disappeared down the hatch into the engine room. Evidently he was going to start up the *Repeat*'s Caterpillar and pump the bilge.

A cloud of black smoke billowed from her exhaust. We watched in amazement as the *Repeat* lunged in reverse. Both mooring lines broke and the schooner headed for the pilings beneath The Galley at half speed. The tide was out and the water level was 15 feet below the floor of the restaurant. We yelled in unison and leaped to our feet, sure that the *Repeat* would knock the pilings out from under the building and drop us into the harbor. Marlus reached the door first, but the night latch was on because the restaurant had closed. Before he could spring the latch, we pushed against him and pinned him to the door.

We felt the building shake and heard the roar of the engine. The lights swung to and fro. Glasses tinkled. Cries of "Open that door!" rang out.

"Back away, give me room," Marlus shouted, fumbling with the latch.

Realizing the problem, those in front slacked off. The door swung open and we poured outside. Last to leave was the white-aproned cook.

We rushed to the railing overlooking the water. The *Repeat* had almost disappeared beneath The Galley. Her stern and most of her pilothouse had been driven under the timbers across the tops of the pilings. Her stack was bent over at a rakish angle, and diesel smoke poured from several places in the ruined exhaust system. Evidently her mast had stopped her as it came against the side of the restaurant.

Jess didn't know, when he started the engine, that the boat puller had left it in gear. He hadn't realized anything was wrong until he climbed the ladder and saw the pilings approaching fast. He tried to get to the wheelhouse controls to throw the engine into forward gear, but he was too late.

Beamy leaned over the rail and surveyed the scene solemnly. Big Jess's bearded face peered out from the back of the pilothouse. Beamy nodded to him and said, "Well, Cap, that's one fast way of putting a galley on deck."

Lituya Bay

Salmon trolling was yielding smaller and smaller catches along the shore off Sitka and the Cape Cross area after World War II. About 1954 a few highline trollers from Pelican began exploring what was reported to be a new ground some 35 to 50 miles off Cape Fairweather. Veteran trollers Toivo Anderson, (now of Sitka), Peter Larsen and Conrad Clippert of Pelican found good salmon fishing. Although they lacked any sure method of locating and holding the banks during those pre-electronic days except by compass, lead line and their own good sea sense, they stuck with it. Their success brought others and before many years had passed a fair-sized fleet was working the Fairweather Ground.

Anyone who trolls for salmon off Cape Fairweather, however, soon finds himself caught in one of the frequent gales that plague the area. It's not uncommon for the weather to be calm along the coast and to find a raging southeaster blowing on the East Bank, only 35 miles out. It's a tough show.

When the wind starts howling and the sea picks up, the fishermen look for shelter. There's not too much choice. Yakutat Bay provides good protection but it lies 75 miles northwest of the grounds. After the gale you're faced with a 75-mile buck into the leftover slop to get back to the fishing. To point your bow into the rapidly rising wind and fight the steep seas to Dixon Harbor, some 70 miles to the east, is not appealing either. Another option is to slip in behind Cape Fairweather. The cape offers some protection, but the anchorage is usually uncomfortable and can become downright dangerous if the wind veers to anywhere from southwest to north, putting the precariously anchored trollers on a lee shore.

That leaves Lituya Bay, as close as Cape Fairweather to the fishing grounds but with an excellent anchorage protected from almost every point. It also has an infamous entrance bar.

Lituya Bay, carved out over the eons by the action of glaciers, penetrates 7 miles into the spectacular Fairweather Range. The bay averages between ¾ and 2 miles in width. In the central part of the bay lies Cenotaph Island. Gilbert and Crillon inlets extend northwestward and southeastward, respectively, from the head of the bay. Gilbert Inlet is nearly filled by Lituya Glacier, as is Crillon Inlet by its namesake, the North Crillon Glacier.

The two inlets lie along the Fairweather Fault, an active source of earthquakes. Steep mountains rise abruptly to 6,000 feet around Lituya Bay, with 12,726-foot Mt. Crillon standing guard at the head of the bay. Close at hand and dominating the entire area is Mt. Fairweather, 15,320 feet in elevation.

On July 2, 1786, the great French explorer, Jean La Perouse, on his voyage of discovery around the world, sighted Cape Fairweather. Later that day his ships, *L'Astrolabe* and *La Boussole,* approached what appeared to be a "very fine bay." He hove to and sent out three boats to investigate the entrance bar. By the time the boats returned with their report, the tide was ebbing, so La Perouse remained hove to for the night.

The following morning the explorer set sail and pointed his ships' bows into the narrow opening on the flood tide. Not being familiar with the bar and its treacherous currents, they had a harrowing crossing. Said La Perouse in his journal, "During the 30 years that I have followed the sea I never saw two vessels so near being lost." Luck was with them, and they safely anchored inside the beautiful bay.

Ten days later they were not so lucky. La Perouse sent three boats out to sound the entrance bar in order to complete his chart of the area. One of the boats was caught in the ebb current and began to be swept toward the breakers. A second boat, and then the third went to its aid. All three were sucked into the dangerous breakers—and only one fought free. Two boats and 21 men were lost.

In memory of the drowned men, La Perouse erected a monument on the island in the bay, and then named it Cenotaph Island. He remained in the bay until July 30, then set sail for California and the South Pacific.

Few bars in ordinary use are as respected today. The inexperienced seaman seeking shelter, should he arrive off Lituya Bay on the ebb with a heavy swell running, may be so terrified at the appearance of the bar that he will decide to either ride out the storm at sea or run with it and take his chances behind the meager protection of Cape Fairweather.

La Chaussee Spit (meaning "The Chopper" in French) at the northwest end of the bar, is actually a steep wall between the deep water of the bay and the Pacific Ocean. The bar has a minimum depth of 33 feet at low water. At high tide the entrance is about 1,000 feet wide, but at low water it is reduced by shallow banks of sand and gravel to 600 feet. If a heavy swell is breaking, the entrance is then reduced to about 150 feet between breakers. The tremendous volume of water which flows into and out of the bay every 6 hours is forced through this narrow entrance, producing, at times, 12-knot currents. A set of range lights and markers on shore assists the helmsman in keeping his boat in the center of the channel, but it is a tricky job even in normal conditions because of the whirlpools, cross currents and tide rips.

When there are very heavy swells, especially from the southwest, the bar breaks clear across, and on an ebb tide it is at its worst. Then it will be a spectacular sight, and no vessel trying to cross would be likely to survive. Oddly enough, however, the velocity of the flood current often knocks down the breaking seas, and entry into the bay can sometimes be made even under severe storm conditions.

Leaving the bay is often much more difficult than entering; it is suicidal to try to ride the ebb current into a breaking swell.

The Laverne II *with her bow to the shore in Lituya Bay, taking on fresh water from a hose that leads to a small creek. In many of Alaska's bays and inlets the water is deep right up to the shoreline.*

Trollers frequently become bar-bound in the bay. Twenty or 25 days out of 30 might be spent inside during the spring.

A few boats have been lost on this bar, and too many lives. There have been innumerable close shaves, usually when boats arrive late and are confronted with the ebb. I've said a few prayers myself, but the worst experience I remember was in April, 1976.

We were on the East Bank, 35 miles offshore, at 8 P.M. on the 25th when the weather told me it was time to head for shelter. We were the only boat out at the time, having just arrived from Sitka. *Eric J, Silvertip, Castaway* and *Bavaria,* discouraged by poor weather forecasts, were awaiting developments in Lituya Bay.

Steve Thatcher of Tacoma, Washington, was my deckhand. We tried to enter the bay about midnight but were too late on the tide to cross the bar and sailed to Cape Fairweather to wait out the change. We dropped anchor at 2 A.M. and I set the alarm for 8:30, allowing plenty of time to reach the bay on the last half of the flood. Weather conditions for crossing the bar would still be marginal.

The Medallion, *owned by Don Wells of Pelican, anchored far up in Lituya Bay. In the background is the Cascade Glacier, at the head of the bay about midway between Lituya and North Crillon glaciers.*

When we tried to break out the deeply buried anchor in the morning, however, the strain parted the winch's drive chain. Repairs were slow because of a rough sea and 35-knot winds in the anchorage. With little anchor chain out we dragged almost 3 miles before we got the repairs made.

The 19 miles to Lituya Bay took 4 hours because of the south-southeast wind and steep seas. The weather forecast was for 40 to 60 knots south of Cape Fairweather and 60 to 80 knots to the north. Two tugs were talking on the radio, one 30 miles outside of Lituya Bay. He reported his wind gauge reading a steady 90, with gusts to well over 100 knots.

We were late on the tide. The bar was impossible. For half an hour or so we jogged in the ebb current coming out from the bar, trying to decide what to do. Steve had never seen Lituya's bar before. Normally as red-faced as any fisherman, his complexion was rapidly changing from red to green and then white as we watched. I could go to Yakutat, 100 miles to the west, or try to fight the steep seas and wind another 30 miles down the coast to Dixon Harbor. I'm not a praying man, but I remember asking a few favors that day. I think I made a few promises, too.

Studying the bar, I counted the interval between breaks. It averaged between 1½ and 2 minutes. Under normal conditions I might have been able to cross in that length of time. But bucking an ebb . . . not a chance.

About the time I had decided to opt for the long, rolling trip to Ocean Cape and Yakutat I happened to take a last look at that bar. I couldn't believe my eyes. A narrow lane now appeared between the breakers along each side. Remembering the unattractive alternatives, I looked seaward to see if any ugly ones were approaching, then swung the wheel and pointed the bow in. I knew there'd be no turning back. That hole wasn't wide enough to trade ends in. Speed on a rough bar is unthinkable and I had to force myself to keep from reaching for the throttle. All I could do was steer and hope.

The noise was deafening. Both of us were on the bridge. I clutched the wheel with my eyes locked on the range markers. Steve watched astern for a breaker, clinging to a pipe with white-knuckled hands.

Suddenly Steve pointed aft. A quick glance confirmed my worst fears. A big break had started just outside the bar, and the ebb was slowing us down. We had only one chance—beat that break in. I opened the throttle as far as it would go. I now really had my hands full keeping the boat from broaching as we dropped nose down in the seas.

Then Steve yelled something in my ear. I thought he yelled, "We've had it!" Clenching my teeth, I waited for that boiling wall of hell to strike the back of my neck. But then I saw he was grinning. I looked back. We were safely inside, and the giant comber was dying just off our stern. What he'd shouted was, "We've made it!"

For a while we jogged just inside and watched the bar. Another, and another huge break swept the narrow entrance. Within a few minutes every sea broke completely across. Why had the bar relented for those few precious minutes? Maybe somebody wanted to see us safely inside.

We were both dead tired, having slept little in the preceding 24 hours. By 6 P.M. we were both in the sack. I remember taking time to thank someone, though, and vowed never again to take such a foolish risk.

The Giant Waves

On the evening of July 9, 1958, eight mountaineers lay resting on the sand on La Chaussee Spit at Lituya Bay. They had just completed the difficult climb of Mt. Fairweather on the Alaska-Canada border. Waiting for a seaplane scheduled to pick them up, they watched with mild interest as a 40-foot troller, the *Edri,* crossed the bar just before 8 P.M. and cruised noisily up the bay. She continued on and anchored in 5 fathoms in a small cove along the south shore behind The Paps, two hills on the broader south shore of the bay near the entrance. A short time later two other trollers, the *Badger* and the *Sunmore,* came in and anchored behind the narrow spit on the north shore near the men.

The seaplane arrived and the alpinists waded out to it, clambered aboard and departed for Juneau. Before the mountaineers had reached their hotel, about 10 P.M., a series of waves, some reportedly more than 100 feet high, swept over the dying embers of their campfire.

Howard G. Ulrich, on the *Edri* with his 7-year-old son, had been tired when they arrived in Lituya Bay and he had gone to bed soon after the anchor was down and holding. Before long he was awakened by a violent rocking of the boat. He went on deck to be greeted by an earthquake in progress in the mountains at the head of the bay. It was just after 10:15 P.M. He witnessed a great shaking and heaving of the land, followed by avalanches.

About 2½ minutes after he first felt the upheaval, a deafening crash resounded from the head of the bay. Then, before his unbelieving eyes, an incredible wall of water rose nearly 2,000 feet up the face of the mountain that blocked the end of the bay. And as he continued to watch, horrified, a giant wave began to move toward him, about 6 or 7 miles away.

110

"The wave definitely started in Gilbert Inlet," Ulrich said later, "just before the end of the quake. It was not a wave at first. It was like an explosion, or a glacier sluff. The wave came out of the lower part, and looked like the smallest part of the whole thing. The wave did not go up 1,800 feet, the water splashed there."

Ulrich raced forward to his anchor winch. The anchor would not break out. Reacting with great presence of mind, he let out all 40 fathoms of chain and started the engine, then turned to watch the rapid approach of the great wave.

Midway between the head of the bay and Cenotaph Island, the wave was a straight wall of water stretching from shore to shore. Ulrich estimated it to be about 100 feet high. As it came around the north side of the island it was breaking, but on the south side of the bay—the side where the *Edri* waited—it had a smooth, even crest. As the monster approached, the wave front appeared very steep and about 50 to 75 feet high. Ulrich could detect no unusual lowering or other disturbance of the water around the boat, other than the vibrations still felt from the earthquake.

Approximately 2½ to 3 minutes after he first sighted the wave, the wall of water reached them and the *Edri* rose up its face. The heavy anchor chain snapped like a piece of string. The boat was carried swiftly toward and probably right over the south shore of the bay by the crest, which Ulrich guessed to be between 25 and 50 feet wide. Then, miraculously, the wave passed under them and the troller and her crew, caught in the backwash, were swept back toward the center of the bay.

After the great wave passed the surface of the bay returned to its normal level. Despite the fact that the water was very turbulent with sharp waves, up to 20 feet high, sloshing back and forth from shore to shore, Ulrich managed to keep the *Edri* under control. In about half an hour the bay became calm. A great many logs covered the water near the shores and began moving first toward the center of the bay and then out the entrance.

At 11 P.M. Howard Ulrich and his son sailed safely out of Lituya Bay on a normal ebb current. The *Edri* was a lucky ship.

When Mr. and Mrs. William A. Swanson entered Lituya Bay aboard the *Badger* at about 9 P.M. they first went in as far as Cenotaph Island, then reversed course to Anchorage Cove on the north shore near the entrance, where they anchored in 4 fathoms of water near the *Sunmore*. The Swansons went to bed as soon as everything was secure.

Then, not long after, like Howard Ulrich, Swanson was awakened by a violent vibration of the boat. He got up to see what was wrong. About a minute later, probably before the end of the earthquake itself, he looked past the north end of Cenotaph Island toward the head of the bay and was presented with an extraordinary sight. He saw what he thought to be Lituya Glacier, which had "risen in the air and moved forward so it was in sight. . . . It seemed to be solid, but was jumping and shaking. . . . Big cakes of ice were falling off the face of it and down into the water."

Shortly after, the "glacier" dropped out of sight, and then Swanson saw a big wall of water roar over the point of land at the southwest end of Gilbert Inlet. Looking over the southern tip of Cenotaph Island, Swanson next saw the tremendous wave lunge high up on the south shore of the bay near Mudslide Creek. As the wave approached the *Badger* past Cenotaph Island, it appeared to Swanson to be about 50 feet high near the center and to slope up higher at the sides.

About 4 minutes after he first sighted it, the wave reached the anchored *Badger*. The 40-foot troller was lifted like a toy and the Swansons were treated to a ride they would never forget. Sweeping stern first just below the crest of the wave like a surfboard, the *Badger* was carried across La Chaussee Spit. As they shot over the tongue of land, Swanson looked down on the trees that grew on the spit. He estimated that the *Badger* rode approximately two boat lengths, or about 80 feet, above the tops of the highest trees!

Aerial photo of Lituya Bay after the giant wave of July 9, 1958. An earthquake in a major fault that runs through the area triggered a massive rockslide from the cliff (A) at the head of the bay. The enormous weight of rock falling into the bay caused a "splash" that rose to an altitude of 1,720 feet up the side of the spur ridge (B) facing the cliff, and then a series of gigantic waves were generated that swept the length of the bay and the adjacent shoreline. The trollers Badger *and* Sunmore *were anchored behind La Chaussee Spit (C) at the entrance. The third boat in the bay that evening, the* Edri, *was anchored at (D) on the south side of the bay.*

Just outside the spit the crest of the great wave broke, the *Badger* struck bottom and shortly after foundered some distance from the shore. The Swansons abandoned their troller, taking to a small skiff, and were rescued by a fishing boat 2 hours later.

The third boat in the bay that night, the *Sunmore,* and her crew was not so lucky. When the wave was sighted they managed to get under way, but they were swamped by the wave near the entrance and the boat and crew were lost.

At the time of the great wave I was trolling in Tebenkof Bay on Kuiu Island, some 200 miles southeast of Lituya, and I didn't feel the quake. As I was fishing, the late Skip Jordan of Petersburg, then owner of the *Nohusit,* passed by and yelled across to me that "a wave 1,800 feet high" had struck Lituya Bay.

That night those of us fishing the area gathered around the buying scow *Point Reyes* and talked of little else than the events in Lituya Bay. At first, reports of the height of the wave were widely doubted; trees and earth swept away from above the 1,000 foot level were attributed to earthslides caused by the quake.

Once the height was confirmed almost everyone had an opinion as to what caused the wave. The most logical reason presented, and the one I found to be the most frightening, was that the fault had opened up, filled momentarily with water, then closed quickly, "squirting" out a tremendous volume of water.

Don J. Miller, a scientist with the U.S. Geological Survey, made a thorough study of the event and published his findings in 1960 in the Geological Survey Professional Paper, "Giant Waves in Lituya Bay Alaska." He determined that the severe earthquake had triggered a massive rockslide, containing 40 million cubic yards (90 million tons) of material, from about the 3,000-foot elevation on the mountainside above Gilbert Inlet, almost adjacent to the face of Lituya Glacier. The gigantic splash which resulted when the slide hit the water climbed to 1,720 feet on the spur ridge across the inlet, sweeping all before it. This in turn generated the great wave, that was found to have averaged 100 feet in height, which traveled toward the mouth of the bay at approximately 100 mph. Miller estimated that the waves removed more than 4 million cubic yards of topsoil from bedrock where it inundated the shore.

Incredible proof of the size of the giant wave, or "splash," that devastated Lituya Bay on July 9, 1958. This spur ridge adjacent to the Lituya Glacier (see point B on the photo on page 113) was denuded of all vegetation to a height of 1,720 feet above sea level.

It wasn't until May, 1963, that I first entered Lituya Bay. The great scars along the shoreline were almost as fresh as if they had just been inflicted. We found places where trees 2 and 3 feet in diameter had been sheared off by the wave and often divided into short lengths, like stovewood. By 1977 the scar was still an impressive sight.

After 1958, a number of fishermen decided not to anchor in the bay any more. It was difficult to sleep soundly, they said. Most of us ignore the threat, but are often reminded of what could happen when slides are heard roaring off the mountain slopes. Giant waves have occurred in Lituya Bay once every 21 to 23 years. By that accounting, another will be due soon.

I hope I'm not anchored there when it happens.

Louie and the 'Valor III'

The Hiram M. Chittenden Locks and the Lake Washington Ship Canal connect Lakes Union and Washington in Seattle with Puget Sound. With the lake levels several feet higher than the level of the sound, the locks allow vessels—tugs and barges, pleasure craft, ships of all kinds, skiffs and fishing boats—to navigate between fresh water and the greenish tidewater of Puget Sound. The locks mark the start and finish of long seasons in Alaska or down the coast for the many commercial fishermen who live and keep their boats in the Seattle area.

Rich in local color and marine atmosphere, the locks are a favorite place for armchair adventurers and tourists. Streaming through the locks in both directions is an almost continual potpourri of watercraft, their sterns frequently bearing the names of home ports other than those on Puget Sound, names such as Friday Harbor, Angoon, Pelican, Lofall, Metlakatla. Sea buffs are fascinated by the boats and by the men and women who sail them to exotic-sounding places. Urbanites, unaware of the fury of the sudden gales, the bitter cold, the damp, cramped quarters and the countless hours of toil on heaving decks without pay, think the seafarers' lives are full of bold adventure and escape.

Early on April 23, 1958, the commercial troller *Valor III,* gleaming with a fresh coat of white paint, entered the locks outbound.

"Off to Alaska for the salmon, Louie?" called out one of the lock attendants.

"No. I used to go up there, but I haven't for years. Can't afford to buy enough warm clothes."

"Ah, go on. All you fishermen are rich."

"That's right," Louie Rogenes replied good-naturedly,

"nothing but easy money in this racket." He handed the passage form to the attendant.

The gates of the lock opened and the *Valor III* moved slowly out to the salt water. She approached the railroad bridge, slipped under the raised span, and speeded up. Louie lowered a starboard window, leaned out and peered up the hill. Only a few blocks away was his house. His wife Gertrude had taken him down to the boat and would be safely back home. Louie's daughter Violet and her family also lived nearby. Each year it became harder to depart, but fishing was the only work Louie cared about or had done since arriving in America from Norway 40 years before.

When the *Valor III* was in the clear, Louie engaged the clutch on his Wood Freeman automatic pilot, locking it to the vessel's steering system. This was Louie's most important piece of equipment. It would steer the boat endlessly without complaint, food or pay. Without it, Louie could not have operated the boat alone. Known as a loner among the fleet, Louie seldom accompanied other boats, preferring to go his own way.

Operating the *Valor III* alone really wasn't as much work as some might think. Louie had built the boat himself, shaping and fitting the planks and timbers with loving care. The vessel was designed so that everything was handy. Steering and throttle were in the stern as well as the wheelhouse. And after many years, Louie had reduced the chores to an absolute minimum. Cleaning the rainbow-colored kings took only a flick of the knife, a toss of the insides to the waiting gulls and a few scrapes with the hose. Meals were simple: lots of fresh fish.

After 10 days, the length of time iced, dressed salmon can be kept, Louie was in Westport on the coast. Fishing had been poor but it was early in the season. The buyers were glad to see the *Valor III*. They knew Louie's fish were of good quality.

After the fish were unloaded and the boat washed out, Louie called home. He told his wife he was in Westport, that he'd do some chores, take on fuel and ice the next day and probably depart the following day. Because salmon fishing was rather poor he planned to work his way down the coast and end the next leg of his trip in Eureka, California. He'd call her from there. Louie said the tuna would be showing soon.

At dawn 2 days later, the *Valor III* crossed Grays Harbor bar and headed south. In Seattle Mrs. Rogenes busied herself with work in the house and garden.

Waiting for a call is the lot of any fisherman's wife. But as the days became weeks and still she did not hear from Louie, Mrs. Rogenes became concerned. Finally, she called the Coast Guard.

When a vessel is listed as missing, there are many facts the officer in charge of search and rescue must consider. The list of reasons why a boat becomes overdue or missing is almost as long as the list of missing boats. Small wooden vessels such as *Valor III* can collide with freighters in fog or darkness without the freighters even being aware of the mishap. Other freighters, fearing the results of a Coast Guard inquiry, have been known to disappear quietly into the night after striking a drifting fishing vessel. Fires can damage the electrical system, preventing a radio message. Large logs are another hazard. Striking a boat squarely, a log can split a boat's bow as if it were a ripe watermelon. And it isn't unusual for a missing boat to be found fishing, with everything under control.

Considering everything, the Coast Guard views new listings with some skepticism and speculation unless there's been a distress signal or other reason to believe something unusual has happened. In the case of the *Valor III*, the Coast Guard's preliminary investigation left little doubt that something was amiss.

Now a monumental effort began. Word was passed to every Coast Guard station along the coast to add the *Valor III* to the dog-eared missing list. A harbor search was initiated and the name of the missing vessel was announced over the airwaves so the fleet could assist in the search.

The gates open at the Hiram M. Chittenden ("Ballard") Locks, Seattle. These busy locks provide access to the salt water of Puget Sound and the Pacific Ocean for the great fleet of commercial fishermen, pleasure boats and other craft that moor in the fresh water of Lakes Union and Washington.

A thousand restless trolling boats tossed and danced in dozens of out-of-the-way harbors along the coast. They were in port for a day or two making turn-arounds or repairs. Into this nomadic fleet of boats, went the young, suntanned enlisted men.

Boats answering the description of the *Valor III* were everywhere, except the names differed. There were boats named after the months of the year, women, sea birds, sea animals, trees and capes along the Pacific coast. Some had more heroic or romantic names. The search turned up the *Valor II,* Louie's old boat, but the captain had no idea of the whereabouts of the missing vessel. Morro Bay, Moss Landing, Sausalito, Bodega Bay, Fort Bragg, Eureka, Brookings, Charleston, Newport,

A quartet of trollers tied up at Westport on Washington's Pacific coast. Westport, with fish buyers on hand, is a convenient base during the season for boats that fish the Pacific grounds.

Astoria, Warrington—all were searched. Along the Washington coast the men looked in Westport, Ilwaco, La Push and Neah Bay. Canadian and Mexican authorities were also involved in the search.

Each time Mrs. Rogenes called the Coast Guard, the answer was the same: "No, there is no news. Yes, everything possible is being done." Still she was hopeful. No true seaman's wife gives up easily.

Then a nor'wester, the kind that drives boats the size of *Valor III* to seek shelter, hit the coast. Each year about July 4, the fleet expects such a storm and the wind seldom fails to strike. In Newport, Oregon, the closest harbor to where most of the fleet was concentrated, boats were lined up 10 deep at the floats. The vessels plunged and bounced even inside the bay. Outside, the dreaded northwest wind moaned and whistled, driving geysers of boiling white foam over the top of the rock jetty. Groups of fishermen cursed the gale that kept them pinned to the floats.

Each noon the albacore fleet observed a silent hour, intended to give any vessel in distress a chance to be heard over 2638. Those with powerful sets—such as Jim Brandenburg on the *Jinita,* Roy Herrington on the *Peso II,* Conrad "Pete" Peterson on the *Sunray II,* or Frank Bohannon on the *Pacific Wave,* or others in strategic positions—also would relay information about prices, missing vessels and where fish were. The *Valor III* was mentioned many times during the silent hour.

By July 10 the storm was over and the fleet was back at sea. Word filtered down the coast by way of radiotelephone that a disaster had struck in Lituya Bay, a wave 100 feet high had sunk two boats and drowned two persons. Tidal wave warnings were announced along the entire coast for any shallow bars and inlets.

The 13th Coast Guard District cannot search indefinitely for a missing vessel. Thousands of square miles of storm-tossed sea cannot be covered, especially with no information on which to base the search. The *Valor III* was a tiny vessel, only visible for a few miles, and it had been missing since the end of May. If the *Valor III* were still afloat, her best chance of being found was by the fishing fleet itself.

To relieve her feeling of helplessness, in August Mrs. Rogenes contacted a local newspaper and offered a reward for information. The newspaper published a brief story the next day.

Finally, early in September the *Valor III* was discovered drifting 300 miles northeast of the Hawaiian Islands by the U.S. Navy submarine salvage ship *Florikan.* Louie's body was found on board, but it was never determined what caused his death.

On a cold and rainy day in Seattle, two trollers, inbound and lashed together, came through the Hiram M. Chittenden Locks. One was a conventional troller. The other boat had been stripped of her mast and tall poles; her paint was streaked with rust and green algae clung to the hull below the water line.

A shout came from the lock attendants. "Well, she's finally home!" They knew the *Valor III.* They had watched her come and go for many years. They had wished her good luck last spring, and they had followed her tragic story in the papers and by word of mouth. They knew she had been found near Hawaii, and

The big Northern California fishing port of Eureka. Many of the Pacific tuna trollers put in here to sell their fish and replenish their ice and other supplies.

they knew Mrs. Rogenes and her daughter Violet had flown to Honolulu to claim her and to arrange for the return of the *Valor III* to Seattle.

Moored among other trollers at Fishermen's Terminal, the vessel attracted many curious people. When it was announced she was for sale, many fishermen came to look. Her sour odor and neglected appearance drove most of them away, doubting that anything could ever remove the stench of rotting fish that had soaked into her wood.

But she was a good boat, and fisherman Cliff Emmet decided he could make her shipshape again. He bought her, rolled up his sleeves and went to work. When spring came and the fleet began to leave for sea, the *Valor III* again slid through the locks. Her mast had been restepped, new fir poles were rigged, her hull gleamed with a fresh coat of paint and her diesel belched blue smoke again.

I first saw the boat in Sitka. Once again she was fighting her old enemies, the wind and steep seas, off Cape Edgecumbe and Point Amelia. Later that summer, trollers along the California coast were mildly surprised to see her hard at work on the albacore grounds.

Today, the *Valor III* still sails for salmon and tuna. The familiar patter of fish tails sounds on her sturdy fir-planked decks while a reliable automatic pilot turns her helm back and forth, keeping the bow pointed in whatever direction her captain wishes to go.

And why not? Wasn't she carefully built by the skilled and loving hands of a man who wanted a sturdy boat, a boat that would take him safely to sea and bring him home again?

Louie Rogenes, the veteran fisherman, would be very proud of his vessel's record, very proud indeed.

The U.S. Navy submarine rescue ship Florikan *which found the* Valor III.

Buzzed by a UFO

It's odd how small experiences sometimes engrave themselves into the brain and thus affect your life forever, while others, seemingly more noteworthy, are eventually forgotten. Everyone has a treasure trove of these mini-happenings on tap, always ready to be brought out and reexamined.

An incident of unusually short duration, which made a lasting impression on me, occurred one balmy night at sea on September 2, 1973. I had left Newport, Oregon, about noon on the *Laverne II*. I was alone and the weather was extra good. I set a course for the tuna grounds offshore, intending to work my way up the Washington coast. Off Cape Foulweather I tossed the jigs out hoping to catch a silver salmon for dinner. Settling back for a long wheel watch, I turned on the radio. It was good to be at sea again after several days in town.

At dusk I took a loran bearing; I was 40 miles west-southwest of Cape Lookout. Not having caught any fish, I pulled the jigs in and decided to run until I got sleepy. Supper was over, the dishes were washed and the galley was tidy. Visibility was good. The lights of Pacific City and other small towns glowed against the sky. Occasionally I walked on deck to stretch my legs and to see that no ships were bearing down on me. A brightly lighted passenger ship was steaming several miles outside of my position. The moon hadn't come up, but the stars glittered overhead. I settled down for another watch, tuned the spare radio to station KWJJ in Portland and relaxed.

Suddenly the radios began to act up. The marine receiver chattered with a noise I'd never heard before. I reached up and changed channels. Then I noticed the citizen's band radio had gone dead.

Glancing out the after door, I noticed the white riding sail on the boom was illuminated by a dim light, like moonlight reflecting off the sea. I paid little attention, assuming that was what it was. What bothered me was the loss of my radios.

The next time I looked aft the sail was a deep red and the light seemed to flicker, as if reflected from a fire. I hurried out the after door and looked for the moon. Instead, I saw a brightly lighted object about 1 mile off my starboard quarter. Its most astounding characteristic was the intense amount of light it radiated. The light pulsated and changed from reddish to golden, then to bluish green and back to a reddish tone again.

The color changes occurred gradually, about a second apart. The smooth surface of the water, my boat and the atmosphere surrounding the object were illuminated by the radiant light. The object appeared to be circular and approaching me directly, descending to about 1,000 feet in elevation. When almost directly astern, the object changed course abruptly. It was at this point that I realized the extraordinary speed at which it was traveling. The object passed close by the stern of the passenger ship, then continued south-southwest.

Probably no more than 20 seconds from when I first saw it, the object disappeared over the horizon. I was so fascinated, however, that I could be mistaken about the length of the observation time. It left a vapor trail and even after it disappeared I could still see a glow in the sky above the horizon.

I wondered if anyone on board the passenger ship had seen it. Ships do not stand by on the voice frequencies, but I dashed into the pilothouse—momentarily forgetting my radio trouble. The transmitter, however, was working normally; the CB was still

The Laverne II *trolling slowly in calm water off the mouth of the Alsek River at Dry Bay, Alaska, between Yakutat and Cape Fairweather. The wind is calm; even the steadying sail is hanging limp.*

dead. (A serviceman later found several burned-out transistors.) My call to the ship went unanswered.

On deck again, I saw that although the vapor trail had dispersed, the glow in the sky, where the object had disappeared, seemed brighter than before. For a few moments I watched, straining my eyes until they watered. Then, quite suddenly, the object reappeared on the horizon. This time it seemed to be traveling straight up. I hurried inside and put a 200mm lens on my camera. I planned to expose plenty of film.

By the time I got back on deck the object had disappeared. I stood there for almost an hour but the sky remained empty. Then I sat down and wrote an account of what had happened: the time, the location, the colors, the electrical interference. Somehow putting the facts on paper helped substantiate what I'd seen.

I also did some simple calculations—an object, 1,000 feet high, disappears over the horizon at a distance of 36 miles. Since the object passed the stern of the passenger ship (about 10 miles away) at less than 1,000 feet, it probably disappeared at about 25 miles. The object's speed was in excess of any aircraft I've observed. The craft, if it was a craft, might have been attracted by the bright lights of the ship. My vessel was also of interest, because the course flown by the object was exactly like that an airplane would choose to "buzz" two vessels at close range for observation.

At 11 o'clock I shut down the engine and crawled into my narrow bunk. Sleep was slow to come. I was certain I'd seen a UFO, and that I had been very close to a being from another planet. This strange feeling lasted many days. Now, I'm not quite so sure. I think if I didn't have the statement I wrote that night, I might discount the whole thing as a dream.

Somehow, after an experience that lasted perhaps 20 seconds, my life will never be quite the same.

The Old Man and the Halibut

Joe Cash was a friendly and sometimes jolly fellow, and he always fished alone in his 36-foot *Flicka*. I first met Joe about 1957 in Tyee, a cold storage and salmon cannery with a small company store, post office, a few company houses and the cannery workers' shacks. Situated in Murder Cove, near Point Gardner on the southwest tip of Admiralty Island, Tyee was once a good fishing location. During the summer Tyee's population swelled to about 50. Winter found only the watchman and numerous brown bears.

Late the following summer I became better acquainted with Joe, down in Tebenkof Bay. A run of fish trickled up Chatham Strait. The salmon would bite for 3 or 4 days on the Tebenkof side, quit, and then for the next few days they'd bite over at Cape Ommaney near Port Alexander. Most of us spent the majority of our time running back and forth trying to outguess the fish.

The shores of Chatham Strait were lined with fish traps. It was always interesting to watch the cannery tenders brail those traps, because enough salmon to put an individual fisherman on easy street for life spilled into the scows within minutes. Even on days when the fish weren't biting for us hook-and-line men, the traps caught fish, a reminder of our inefficiency.

At the time I had a small boat, an 18-foot inboard with an 8- by 4-foot cabin. My narrow bunk was wedged alongside the air-cooled Wisconsin engine. I could lie in bed on cold mornings, reach the hand crank, spin it to start the engine, then submerge under the covers until the cabin was warm. Because of my cramped quarters, other trollers often took pity on me and invited me aboard their boats on harbor days or in the evenings, especially when the weather was unpleasant.

Joe Cash was no exception. He was a smallish, red-faced man who kept himself and his boat neat. He usually wore bib overalls, somewhat of an oddity among fishermen who are Frisco jeans and woolen pants fans. Perhaps Joe's "farmer pants" were a holdover from his younger days on a Dakota farm.

One rainy evening Joe and I sat at his tiny fo'c'sle table drinking coffee. Talk got around to the boats that had already departed for town, claiming they were quitting for the season. Suddenly Joe stood up, went to his bunk and felt around the edge of his mattress. He put a jar of money on the table.

"I've been wanting to count up and see how much I've made," Joe said, fumbling under the mattress again. "If I've made enough, I'm heading for Petersburg tomorrow. Then I'm going to Seattle, put *Flicka* in her stall, and go to Dakota for some pheasant hunting."

"Looks like you've robbed a bank. How many more of these jars are hidden up there?"

"Half a dozen. My name ain't Cash for nothing."

"How much money do you think there is?"

"No idea," Joe said. "Hell, by the time I unload, clean up, eat and get the dishes washed, I'm so sleepy I just tumble into bed."

Joe sat down and began sorting and smoothing out the bills.

I watched. More money lay on that table in front of me than I'd ever seen at one time. I think my complexion turned slightly green, because Joe looked at me sharply.

"Well, don't just sit there. Help me count this mess," he growled, turning a jar of cash out before me.

We smoothed and stacked the bills. Many hundreds were mixed in, and, of course, there were lots of silver dollars, which were common in Alaska before statehood. When we had everything stacked, the table was covered.

"How much is enough?" I asked.

"My mind's made up. If there's $7,500, I'm through." Joe found some paper and a pencil. "I'll count. You write down the figures."

After the figures were written down, I left Joe bent over the paper, adding them up, and went on deck for some fresh air. We were anchored at Troller Islands. The spruce-covered shore was but a few feet away. Half a dozen boats swung on their anchors. Over on the *Point Reyes,* the big buying scow, several lights gleamed. Although it was almost 10 P.M., it was still daylight. I looked at the western sky. The low-hanging clouds were not moving. The southeast wind, which had kept us harbor-bound all day, had stopped. Hopefully, I'd be able to get out again tomorrow. Few fish were inside the protected bay. To catch them, one had to venture several miles out into the strait. Skip Jordan and his big *Nohusit* had come in and tied to the scow only an hour ago. We'd watched him unload, counting the fish as they were tossed by hand onto the scow. He had 32 kings and silvers. The *Nohusit* was anchored alongside now, its cabin dark.

I couldn't get all that cash off my mind. There was money to be made in the trolling business if one had a suitable boat. But how did one make enough money with a small boat to buy a boat large enough to make money?

Joe's whoop called me back to the galley. "You made it."

"With money to spare."

"That's great. Wind's gone down. You should have good traveling weather."

"I'll be in Petersburg late tomorrow night. How about you?"

"I'm going to be fishing a while longer."

"Well, so long. Thanks for helping count."

"Have a good hunt. It's always a pleasure to count money, even someone else's. See you next spring on your way through Ketchikan."

Joe liked to operate around Petersburg, Frederick Sound and Chatham Strait. You seldom saw the *Flicka* outside. Joe's favorite spot was the tiderip around Point Gardner, a miserable place to troll. Sea conditions are seldom good because of the ebb

The halibut boat Keku Queen, *moored at the Petersburg Public Cold Storage wharf at the head of Wrangell Narrows, Alaska. These boats are the troller's companions on the fishing grounds in season. The anchors hanging on the stern are used to hold the ends of the long halibut lines to the bottom and the big balloonlike buoys hold the upper ends and mark the positions of the lines on the surface.*

tide converging hell-bent down the two mighty waterways. The resulting tiderip is given a wide berth by seafarers with local knowledge. There is not only shallow ground in the area, but great, twisted masses of bull kelp and logs gather in the rips and threaten to strip the troll leaders off the main lines. I once asked Joe why he still fished there when most everyone else had given it up as not worth the trouble.

"Well," Joe admitted, "it is a miserable place and I lost a lot of lead until I learned the lineups. But whether it's halibut or salmon, Point Gardner produces some whoppers. And I'd rather catch one 50-pounder than five 10-pounders anytime. I'm just lazy, I reckon."

Joe had the halibut spots figured out, too. He knew where to be at different stages of the tide, and his visual sightings on points, islands and rocks steered him safely through the reefs. One lineup he used often was the roof of the cannery building. In this area the fish generally fed only during part of the tide, so Joe knew when to be out fishing and when he could relax on the anchor in Murder Cove. This gave him time to cook, to clean and ice his fish, and take a nap.

Later I managed to buy a boat large enough to fish outside. I didn't see much of Joe after that—usually we had Baranof Island between us—but I often heard him on the radio. One day he was complaining that Tyee, which had been closed for several years, was being torn down. That meant Joe was losing one of his most important lineups. Still, he hung on around Point Gardner, sometimes venturing down the strait to Port Alexander and to the west sides of Kuiu and Kupreanof islands.

One day late in the summer of 1974 Joe, now 67, was fishing in Frederick Sound, off Kupreanof Island's Eagle Point. He hooked a halibut big enough to give two men a bad time. With their powerful tails, halibut have smashed small skiffs, stove in planks, broken oars and seats, and bruised many a man. Worse yet, they can be shot or clubbed into unconsciousness only to come thrashing back to life minutes, or even hours, later.

The standard method of handling large halibut is with a shark hook and short piece of line. As soon as the fish comes to the surface, and before it breaks the 120-pound nylon leader, the fisherman slips the shark hook into the fish's mouth or head. This results in a display of brute strength as the alarmed fish flails about in the water. The troll leader is usually broken in the process, but if the shark hook has been well placed and the short rope holds, the fish settles down enough so the fisherman can either club it or shoot it in the head. Even then it is often led around the stern and tied to a cleat or pole until it is quiet enough to be brought on board.

Baiting up the sturdy hooks on the halibut lines. Many hooks are attached to each carefully coiled line, and every hook must be kept extremely sharp.

Vaughn Wilson cleans a medium-sized halibut aboard the Laverne II. *These powerful fish have to be handled carefully; a big one can be dangerous if hauled on deck while still alive.*

This particular halibut was about 150 pounds, but Joe expertly placed the shark hook and fired several shots from his .22-caliber pistol into the fish's tiny brain. Then, in order to ease the task of hauling his prize aboard, Joe led it around the side to a spot on the main deck between the hatch and the trolling cockpit. Bracing himself, Joe heaved. The fish slid quietly over the rail and into one of the several landing pens on the deck, each constructed of 2x12 planks turned on edge to keep the fish from escaping.

Joe's halibut would be worth more than $100. He reached down to retrieve the shark hook, and as he worked it loose, the halibut came back to life. Its enormous tail caught Joe off guard. He lost his balance and his booted feet flew out from under him in the halibut slime on deck. Joe landed on his back across two of the upright planks. His head struck the winch and he blacked out.

The maddened halibut now slammed both head and tail into the unconscious man's body. Joe's legs took the full brunt of the onslaught because they were resting across the edge of the plank. He was severely beaten. Several ribs were broken and the bone in his right leg was shattered. The jagged end of bone severed an artery and Joe's blood poured forth, mixing with that of the halibut.

Revenge satisfied and strength gone, the great fish gasped and died.

When Joe regained consciousness, he tried to sit up but the pain in his chest and legs was too much. Within a few feet was the radio—if only he could crawl to it. At least 10 boats were in the area and someone would come to his aid quickly. On his stomach Joe inched along the deck between the winch and the cabin.

Then he came up to the anchor chain. It was wound around the winch capstan and led, a foot or so above the deck, toward the block on the rail beside the cabin. Try as he might, Joe couldn't pass his body under the chain or raise himself high enough to crawl over it. The only way he could reach the cabin and the radio was to crawl around the entire hatch. It was only about 12 feet around to the open door, but he would have to lift himself over several pen boards in the process. From his position on the deck, those 2x12's now loomed above his head like fences.

Joe twisted around to start off in the new direction. From the bottom of his oilskin-covered right leg he left a trail of blood.

The Donna C *in Lituya Bay with her halibut gear aboard. The bamboo poles with the cylindrical floats are halibut flagpoles that are set in the water as markers, attached to the ends of the long lines so that the lines may be easily found again.*

The *Flicka* drifted, her engine idling, out toward the center of the strait as dusk descended. The blood-soaked man inched on. Each plank was an Everest, and each sapped his strength as he dragged his shattered leg over their edges. In one pen were a few smaller halibut tossed there earlier in the day. He pulled his body across the fish, on and on to the last board.

Now it was totally dark. The cabin door was but a few feet away. Pulling himself painfully along, he passed the hatch combing and came to the winch. And there, against that cold steel on which he had first struck his head, Joe remained. He could move his arms, but he had no more strength to drag his body.

Groping around, his hand found a length of rope. He pulled on it until several feet were coiled against his chest. Joe knew he was not going to reach the radio. The *Flicka* might drift out Chatham Strait into the open sea and disappear without a trace, or go onto one of the jagged offshore rocks and reefs that abound in the area. Slowly he fastened the rope around his shoulders and the winch, and tied the final knot. He and the *Flicka* had suffered and depended upon one another for too many years to be separated now.

Joe dropped off into the long, long sleep. A light rain washed over him, and when the rain stopped, his face gleamed white and still in the starlight.

By dawn the *Flicka* had drifted toward Eagle Point, where the shoreline is rugged. Many cliffs hang over the water, and if the *Flicka* had been grounded under one of these, it is likely her fate would never have become known. But instead, like the dependable vessel she was, she pointed her bow toward a sloping beach and hung there while the tide ebbed.

At low tide she heeled so far over that Joe's body probably would have tumbled over the side if he hadn't tied himself down. When the tide turned, *Flicka*'s stern failed to lift because of the angle at which she lay on the beach; the boat partially filled with water.

She was found by a seining crew the next day, her engine still idling, the huge halibut still in the pen. The final story of Joseph T. Cash, could be read on the troller's deck.

The halibuter Leeward *is dwarfed by the great bulk of Mt. Fairweather, symbolic of the sometimes overwhelming power of the forces of nature that the fisherman must challenge every day.*

Epilogue
The Price of Fish

by Ben Hur Lampman from *The Portland Oregonian*

The deep-sea fishing boat *Republic* will never sail out for the tuna again, nor the salmon — out of Astoria into the green swells from westward. Part of her port bow has drifted ashore near Long Beach, and some of the forward deck — and where the hulk of her is, only the sea can tell. Her last port of call was the storm. And the fishermen who sailed her, and looked to her fishing gear, and harvested the sea? Where are they? Perhaps the gulls know, or the cormorants. Only this seems certain — that they and their boat will fish no more.

You walk through the market and glance at the fish stall heaped with limp silver. Only a day or so ago these fish, most of them, were out where "the low sky mates with the sea." Now they bear price tags. Even fish, so we say, is high priced. That is true. Fish are high priced — and the least of the price is reckoned in coin.

Men who would rather fish at sea than work ashore sail out on the fishing boats to seek and follow the fish. It is a glad, hard life, and they like it well — but they stake their lives on the catch. It isn't often that the boats don't come back to port, for their oil-skinned skippers and crews to shout to their friends on the dock with word of their luck — but sometimes they don't. The *Republic* was one that didn't. And how are you going to figure that into the price of a pound of fish?

Glossary

BANK—Shallow offshore ground, usually less than 50 fathoms deep, where extensive fishing is done.

BEACH—The shore, or the area adjacent to the shore; the land.

BELL—The bell on the trolling gear used to indicate when a fish hits. Navigational buoy containing a bell that rings as a result of the movement of the buoy in the sea.

BINNACLE—The case or stand that supports the compass.

BLINKER—Navigational light which blinks on and off.

BOAT PULLER—Deckhand, whose principal task is to pull fishing gear and fish aboard.

BOW POLE—Trolling pole mounted on the bow.

BREAKER—Breaking wave, usually on a shallow bar or beach.

BROKER—A fishing trip which fails to show a profit.

CATHEAD—Fitting at boat's bow to which anchor is hoisted and secured; often a roller on modern boats.

CHOP—Short, rough sea caused by wind or tide.

CLEANING TROUGH—Wooden trough used to hold fish upright while being cleaned.

CLOTHESPIN—Device used to attach tagline to trolling wire.

COCKPIT or PIT—Trolling hatch in deck where man stands to operate gear.

COMBER—A large breaking wave.

CROSSTREE—That part of the mast which supports trolling poles while poles are in the upright position.

CUTTLEFISH—Plastic lure used behind flasher on trolling line.

DOGLINE—Trolling wire suspended by float and towed far behind.

DOWN HILL—The direction of the wind and sea.

DOWNWIND—The direction toward which the wind is blowing.

DRAG—An area frequented by trollers year after year.

DRAG BOARD—Three-cornered piece of plywood dragged astern to slow down a boat.

DROP THE PICK—Let go the anchor.

EBB—Outgoing tidal flow.

EDGE, THE—Can be the outside edge of the fishing bank, where it dops off into the deep. Also can be any depth along a bank, such as the 40-fathom edge.

FATHOM—A measure of water depth equal to 6 feet; sometimes used as a measurement of line or chain.

FATHOMETER—Electronic instrument for measuring water depth.

FEATHERS—Feathers used in construction of a lure to catch tuna.

FENDER—Old tire or other device used to protect side of boat.

FIDDLER—Small fish.

FIRE CRACKER—Small herring used behind flasher.

FISHING GEAR—That part of lines, leaders and other equipment which is lowered into the sea to catch fish.

FLASHER—Chrome device used to attract fish. Used at end of leader, with either bait or plastic "hootchie" behind.

FLAT ONE—Halibut.

FLOAT—Device used to float wire and lead behind boat.

FLOOD—Incoming tidal flow.

FLOPPER STOPPER—Stabilizer hung on pole overside to reduce boat's roll.

FO'C'SLE—Forecastle. Forward compartment, usually serving as crew's living quarters.

GAFF—Hooked tool used to club and lift fish into boat.

GAFF HATCH—Trolling hatch. Where operator stands.

GRABBY BOTTOM—Rocky bottom where leads are easily lost.

GULLEY—Undersea canyon.

GURDIE—Power-operated reel or winch upon which trolling wire is hauled in or out and stored. Sometimes operated by hand on small boats.

GUT—A narrow passage between rocks or islands. To clean and dress fish.

HAUL OUT—Drydock boat.

HAUL-UP—Line which raises and lowers trolling poles.

HIGHLINER—Good producer.

HOLD-DOWN—Device which keeps trolling poles from flying up when boat rolls.

HOOTCHIE—Any of many plastic lures used behind flasher on a trolling line.

HOT SPOT—Area where the fish are biting. Also the trade name of a Canadian plastic flasher and spoons.

JIG—A hand-held device to catch bottom fish; a feathered lure to catch albacore tuna.

JILL POKE—A type of bow pole which is fastened to the main trolling pole.

JIMMY—G.M.C. diesel engine much favored by trollers.

JOGGING—Moving at the slowest possible engine speed, while still retaining steerage way.

KELP BALL—Ball of floating kelp which can foul trolling gear and strip off spreads and lures.

KELPER—Small boat which fishes primarily close to the kelp or the shore.

KNOT—A measure of speed. One knot is one nautical mile per hour.

LEADER—Monofilament leader. Line used to connect lure to trolling wire.

LEE—The side away from or sheltered from the wind.

LONG FIN—Albacore tuna.

LONGLINE—A long length of line or wire to which a series of hooks are attached on spaced leaders.

LORAN—Electronic long range navigation instrument used offshore to establish exact position.

MAIN HATCH—Access hatch into the main hold.

MAIN POLE—Amidships pole.

MARKER—Stop attached to stainless steel trolling wire at 4- or 5-fathom intervals. The stop keeps snaps from sliding, and also indicates the depth.

MICKEY MOUSE—Citizen Band radio.

MUG UP—Coffee in the comfort of the galley.

OFFSHORE—Out on the open ocean, usually too far out to return to anchorage in a harbor at night.

PARACHUTE—Parachute rigged in water off bow to keep bow into wind at night. Used as a sea anchor.

PASS—Narrow channel or passage between islands. To make a pass or cruise in a line across the fishing banks.

PILOT—Automatic pilot that steers a boat at a set compass course without the need of a helmsman. Also called an Iron Mike.

PINNACLE—Sharp underwater peak or rock.

PIT—Trolling hatch.

QUEER ONE—A dangerous or "maverick" sea different from the rest.

RECORDER—Depth indicator that plots a continuous record of the depth of water on a special roll of graph paper.

REEFER—Refrigeration system.

RIDING SAIL—Sail rigged along vessel's boom to reduce roll.

SCOTTY—Plastic float used as a fender and as a longline float.

SCRAPER—Tool used to remove backbone blood from salmon or halibut.

SCREECHER—Jargon for a hard blow; a storm.

SCUPPER—Deck drain hole that allows water to run off the deck.

SET ADRIFT—Stop the engine and let the vessel find her own way.

SHAKE—What a pole does when a salmon strikes.

SHAKER—Undersized salmon which is tenderly released.

SILVER—Coho salmon.

SLOP—Choppy seas.

SMILEY—Salmon large enough to bring top price per pound.

SNAP—German silver device used to snap leader to wire.

SNUBBER—Rubber shock absorber moulded onto snap, intended to reduce strain on monofilament leader when a large salmon strikes.

SOAKER—Large salmon.

SPOON—A type of lure for catching salmon.

SPREAD—The snap, leader and lure. Also used to indicate the distance between line stops, such as 5-fathom spread.

SPRING SALMON—Chinook that spawns in springtime as opposed to one that spawns in the fall.

STRIP—Cut of herring used as bait behind flasher.

TAG LINE—Wire or line attached to end of trolling pole. The lower end is cut to reach the trolling hatch. When the desired depth is reached, a clothespin is fastened quickly to the lower end of the wire. The gurdie is then slacked off until the tagline takes the full weight of the bight of wire.

TUBE—Any radio.

WASH ROCK—An underwater rock which bares at low tide.

WAYS—Marine railway used to haul out boats.

WHIP—A type of antenna mounted on top of the mast.

WHISKEY LINE—A hand-hauled short line fastened usually to the end of the boom, containing a lure which runs near the surface. Profits from such a line can also be used to buy ice cream, and other special goodies.

WHISTLER—Navigational buoy with a whistle activated by the movement up and down of the buoy.

WILLIWAW—Strong, often violent gusty wind which comes over steep mountains or out of mountain valleys and strikes the water close by the shore.